ENI

Knowing my wife, these _ you are about to read is direc_____ ____ _____ enjoys a deep daily relationship with our Lord that many of us wish to also experience on a regular basis. If you have had the opportunity to communicate with God, then you know most of the time God provides thoughts, plans, and direction in "lump sum," seemingly disjointed and convoluted, but usually in its entirety. Much of what follows are some of those communications with Him, collectively gathered as He delivered them.

I encourage you to read these gifts as if you were sitting at her feet, snuggled up in a big comforter, in front of a sparking fireplace. Allow her message, based on His Word, to encompass and embrace you as though she were reading them lovingly to you.

—Richard Sherriff

Denise Sherriff has been known as a mentor, a teacher, a shoulder to cry on, a best friend, a godly woman, but to me, she has always been first and foremost my mother. Growing up, it was amazing watching her connect and have a natural affinity for people, and I knew as I got older that her talent would allow her to do great things. When I heard she was writing a book, I was ecstatic; because I know without a doubt that if this book reflects only a sliver of who she is, it will connect with and give insight to those reading it. I am immensely proud to call Denise Sherriff my mother, and I hope this book brings joy to all who read it.

—Anthony Sherriff

Wow, Denise! This has to be one of the most terrific life-observation/devotional-style collections of thoughts I've read. Had I looked through this writing in the bookstore without knowing you personally, I would still have wiped tears away, and then smiled moments later.

—Patrick Kelley

I have known Denise personally for more than 25 years, and I have grown more and more excited as I watch her continue to grow in her relationship with God and with others.

When we first met, she had come to attend our "Bondage to Freedom" life-change program. Watching her become increasingly more solid in her walk with God, and watching Him do a wonderful healing work in her life was awesome. As her hurt went away, I began to see who she really was. It was like seeing my very own daughter grow up to be a powerful young woman. I am very proud of her.

It was special to observe her falling in love with Richard (Dick), getting married and starting a life together. When their son, Anthony, came along, Denise blossomed, not only into a wonderful wife, but also a truly exceptional mother. I could see that her fulfillment was truly in her family, which made her heart full.

I am sharing this, because as I read her book, it brought back all the special moments I watched her go through. I truly love the way she keeps life simple and all about relationships. She has a special gift that draws people to her, because she has a special relationship with God.

Also, as I read her book, I could not put it down. I found myself involved in each event. It was exceptional. Denise has a unique way of making things real. I think anyone could relate and find true hope and excitement about living life on this planet.

So, I say to her, "Great job, girl! Keep writing, because you truly do have a gift. Your joy and excitement is contagious. This world needs that kind of reality and touch from God. Go Girl!"

—Your Adopted Dad, Ed Glaspey
Founder and Director of Restoration Ministries
www.Restoration.Net

I have known Denise Sherriff for 25 years and count it a privilege to call her my friend. The clearest and most encouraging thing I can say about Denise, is that she lives out what is in her heart. She is truly a person that "practices what she preaches." Her integrity is unquestionable; her love for her family is unmatched; but most important is her love and commitment to the Lord, which is exceptional. When she has passion for something, she is unwavering in her pursuit of the plan of God. I highly recommend to you this woman of God, Denise Sherriff.

—Doug Easterday
Speaker, Author, and Pastor
www.fatherheartofgod.com

Denise Sherriff's inspirational book, *Kairos Moments,* is the type of book that will bring readers a refreshing enthusiasm for renewing, reviving, and reenergizing their relationship with Christ by looking at the moments when God has surely been right beside them, opening doors He wants them to walk through and closing others. Denise takes us along on her journey while helping us to recognize His hand at every turn. He has greater plans for us than we can even imagine. Let this book help you to recognize His hand and trust His plan.

—Yvonne Conte
Author: *Cry, Laugh, Cook!*
www.yvonneconte.com

Kairos Moments demonstrates how beautiful life can be when it is Christ-centered, saturated with prayer, and guided by the Word of God under the influence of the Holy Spirit. Most impressive is the insight and wisdom, Denise displays in relating to those she is mentoring. Nuggets of inspiration are scattered throughout this book. On various occasions, the readers find themselves in the same situations Denise is describing. Your life will be enriched through the truth presented in *Kairos Moments.* In fact, this book will remind you of parables; and of Short stories, easy to remember and potentially life-changing. *Kairos Moments* offers good preparation for more difficult trials that will come.

—Homer G. Rhea
Former Editor in Chief, Pathway Press
CEO, HGR Editorial Services
homer8238@gmail.com

KAIROS MOMENTS

KAIROS MOMENTS

Your life isn't being pillaged and plundered.
It's being shaped and molded
with every opportunity.

By Denise Sherriff

Derek Press
Cleveland, TN 37311

Printed in the United States of America.

ISBN-13: 9781545606247

Dedication

My life is as it should be, because God has never abandoned me. My husband, Richard, and my son, Anthony, are the most celebrated treasures with which God could have ever blessed me. The greatest of all possible honors of which God chose me to be the recipient, is the extraordinary gifts they are. Blessed beyond measure, I do not take lightly the responsibilities of being a wife and mother. I dedicate this book to them with all my love.

> Then Solomon stood before the altar of the LORD in the presence of all the assembly of Israel, and spread out his hands toward heaven (1 Kings 8:22).

Table Of Contents

Foreword

If I were asked to use one word to describe Denise, it would be heart. I know of nothing in life that defines a person more than the heart, and I know no one with a heart more open than Denise. In the Book of Proverbs, we read: "Keep and guard your heart with all vigilance and above all that you guard, for out of it flow the springs of life" (Proverbs 4:23 AMPC).

Life has an array of moments and seasons that are often referred to as life-altering experiences. Whether it's a betrayal of trust, physical challenges, unforeseen uprooting, bouts with depression, or heartbreak (and the list goes on), all these things have the potential of negatively altering our lives. For the hearts that are guarded and remain submitted, these moments and seasons don't destroy them; instead they refine and define them.

I've had the privilege of being Denise's friend for several decades. I have stood with her and watched as she allowed her guarded heart to determine her life-course, rather than allowing the course of her life to be altered by overwhelming circumstances. Being her friend, I know what you will find in these pages will be an oasis for your heart.

By the time you're finished reading this, you will feel like Denise is your new best friend. Her openness, vulnerability, humor, and compassion will refresh you. This book is not a self-help book, but it is a book about the One who is always there to help.

—Pastor David Kauffman
Facetofaceministries.kauffman@gmail.com

Preface

Kairos (pronounced *ki-ross*) moments don't happen with specific sets of details, nor can we plan them. I am reminded of a time when I used a handwritten address book. My son, needing to make a call, was looking up the phone number of a friend. He came to me quite bewildered and asked me: "Mom, why isn't this address book in alphabetical order under each letter heading?" I replied, "Because we don't meet people in alphabetical order." That being said, within the pages of this book, my drawings of the alphabet letters are placed throughout. I have done this as a reminder for you to anticipate God's random order often within structural dimensions on purpose. In Exodus 9:16, we read, "But indeed for this purpose I have raised you up, that I may show My power in you, and that My name may be declared in all the earth."

The sun may be shining, or we may be experiencing a storm; it makes no difference. We experience them as God moves, intermingling our lives among all humanity. *Kairos* is an ancient Greek word meaning, "appropriate opportunity, season, or fitting time." Maybe like you, I've imagined a book that reveals how every event in life is supposed to happen—like when, where, or why. Thinking back on the momentous days of our children's births would have been an ideal time to receive one of those books, for sure!

Do you have a desire to deepen relationships with genuine consideration? Are you able to rejoice in a friend's blessings; or with the same kind of enthusiasm, cry with them during hurting times? Do you look inward before you point to another's behavior? Within these pages, I share personal experiences of how to visualize and understand why embracing God's kairos moments can change your perspective one day at a time. Being able to laugh and cry about my life has helped lighten my burdens, enabling me to give joy away no matter what.

Procrastination and insecurity kept me from writing for many years. As I changed my mindset and began to pray more seriously, God did something amazing. My best friend sent me publishing information from Xulon Press to peruse, and along with that, I received blogs from their Author's Center. One day I was looking for one of the text messages to read and could not find it anywhere. In a few moments, our home landline phone rang, and it was the senior publishing consultant from the publishing company! Who calls on a landline anymore? Most people don't even have one these days. My friend had never given anyone my personal information, and I had NEVER contacted the publishing company. I recalled something God impressed upon my heart many years ago. He said, "Answer the phone, answer the door, and answer your e-mail. Something will happen." No longer could I be disobedient and call myself inadequate, because after all, He asked only that I be willing. So I began.

This book was birthed from my prayer journals for family and friends. This is the most important act of worship for me. One of my most heartwarming assignments for a number of years has been to pray for a dear friend, Deven Wallace, who is co-pastor alongside her husband, Pastor Kevin Wallace, of Redemption to the Nations Church in Chattanooga Tennessee rttnchurch.com. I ask God what Deven needs and listen for His guidance. Deven is also the founder of The Zion Project which brings awareness and activation in regard to the war on sex trafficking and the rescue of women and children www.thezionproject.net.

If we aren't able to do anything else, I believe we are quite able to embrace opportunities with a heart of servitude. With the utmost sincerity, I am praying you will garner encouragement. Certainly, there are days we want to cover up our heads and remain in bed. Other days, we plop our feet on the floor with a bound and are ready for anything. Either way, the day is, without exception, set in motion with a continual ticking of the clock.

How will you spend your time—a most precious commodity? View all that is set before you with inspiration. Avail yourself with the fruit of the Spirit, and clothe yourself with the full armor of God. Give your shoes of peace an extra tug of tightening; greet each day with the highest of hopes, because remember the sun rises without fail. I implore you, seize your day!! Then like clockwork, the setting of the sun comes 'round, signaling the day's end. Surely you will soak in the events of the day's investments with joy, and then rest well.

Therefore, as we have opportunity, let us do good to all, especially to those who are of the household of faith (Galatians 6:10).

But the fruit of the Spirit is love, joy, peace, forbearance, kindness, goodness, faithfulness, gentleness and self-control. Against such things there is no law (Galatians 5:22-23 NIV).

—Denise Sherriff
Website: kairosmoments2017.com
E-mail: kairosmoments2017@yahoo.com
Facebook: facebook.com/kairosmomentsbook

Acknowledgments

I am so blessed to be surrounded by people who are deeply committed to the principles I hold dear.

- Among those people, my husband, Richard, is at the top of the list. My heart is full and grateful for him. There is truly no one else who could put up with me. He never ceases to amaze me and is a rock firmly planted always by my side with his biblical, Berean mindset. He is my hero.
- My precious son, Anthony, is like a crown on my head. He continues to be a shining star in my life that reminds me how faithful God was in answering my prayers to give birth to a son. Thank you, for allowing me to make reference to you throughout this book.
- I thank my sister, Doris, who has been a second mother to me, and I cannot imagine where I would be without her presence in my life.
- A special thanks to my brother, Donnie, who is the bravest man I have ever known. He has voluntarily defended our country with a military career serving in Special Ops.
- I also give remembrance to another sister, Patricia, who is now in her heavenly home, who had a remarkable influence in my life.
- I thank my parents who believed in hard work and wanted their children to do well in life and enjoy the many things they never had opportunity to do. They taught me that relationship was something from the heart no matter where you were from or what color your skin is. I love and appreciate everyone in my irreplaceable and unconventional family, because they are the whole of my roots.
- I'm grateful to my dear friends with whom I have weathered life side by side; I'm also grateful to my prayer partners and ladies of accountability who remind me to dream.

- Thank you to my fabulous daughters; Jennifer, Crissy and Amy for the privilege of being your "Mom Denise." You enlarged my heart from day one.
- To those whom I am a spiritual mother, you are a ray of sunshine to me. My relationship with you brings a fresh vibrancy to my spirit.
- My friend, B.L. Kelley, whose cup overflowed with wisdom and joy; time in a library will never be the same without him. One of his passions was his library and sharing the value we should have for books. One could never pass his door that he would not invite you in for a visit. I will never forget how he read his manuscripts to me as he was writing them while sitting back in his big chair wearing his cowboy hat.
- I am wholeheartedly blessed by my best friend, Denise Cummins, whose help and support made publishing possible and not just a dream.
- Words cannot express the gratitude I feel for my spiritual parents, Ed and Mona Glaspey, who took me under their wing by rescuing me from living in a storeroom to finally following God's plan; as mine had not worked out too well.
- I've made new friends in the realm of book writing, and I so appreciate what my Editor, Homer Rhea, with his amazing staff have done. I'm also thankful for my publisher Xulon Press and the incredible people that answered a plethora of questions as we were all in pursuit of presenting something pleasing to God.
- My heart is full and grateful that I serve a God who does not waste any hurts or pain I have experienced. Those trials have played an invaluable part in transforming me into a God-fearing woman of encouragement today. And to Him, I acknowledge the heart of my faith.

In all your ways acknowledge Him, and He shall direct your paths (Proverbs 3:6).

Also your descendants shall be as the dust of the earth; you shall spread abroad to the west and the east, to the north and the south; and in you and in your seed all the families of the earth shall be blessed (Genesis 28:14).

Introduction

Denise Sherriff is the kind of friend who likes it best when she can sit close to you, look you in the eyes, and have a conversation. So, when she moved 2,500 miles away from me that became difficult!! It would also be difficult for her to have that kind of deep friendship with everyone she knows and every reader of this book. However, I think you will get a good glimpse at the heart of a woman who desires to sit with you and honestly share what God has taught her through a life of twists and unexpected turns. Because of her love for face-to-face conversation and quality time, she comes to life on a higher level when assignments to mentor are sent her way. She recognizes God's Word is full of wisdom and is excited when able to point others in the direction of His kingdom. The insight God has given her was meant to be shared so that you will be drawn closer to your heavenly Father.

—Denise Cummins

Chapter 1

The Opportunity of Offense

We all have the same opportunity anyone else has to rise above any hurt, offense, abuse, or criticism. If we don't, we become stranded like a car stuck in mud. I've found myself in that predicament several times. Mud has a relentless grasp, and what I accomplished trying to free my car was only to bury the tires deeper until help arrived. Our thoughts get stuck like that and make us feel stranded in a frozen-like state of mind. We spin our wheels, yet don't get anywhere; it just seems like we're moving. Either we remain motionless or dig ourselves deeper into a hole, which can seem like we're abandoned. So what do we do? The above mentioned choices don't seem to be very good ones. It's important to be open to the idea that I may be at fault for the pickle I'm in. Blaming others for my predicament won't liberate me. What I need to do is find the correct momentum and method to get out of where I'm stuck. You might literally need a tow truck, but either way, remember, God's Word says He will not abandon us.

The better approach is to choose to believe God's Word, confess God's Word, do what God's Word says, and trust Him. Know who you are in Christ, and be forgiving toward others. If you don't, it's like drinking poison and expecting someone else to die. That may sound like a rash statement, but unforgiveness is harsh and deadly. That's why God tells us to forgive without exception. Others are often unaware that they have even hurt us.

Help is always on the way, if we let God contend with those who contend with us (see Isaiah 49:25). The Lord says we must forgive others, or He won't forgive us. So we must not allow doubt to roam freely in our heads. We will get stuck every time in what I call clutter of the mind. If you have a difficult time believing what His Word says, repeat it until you do believe it! God is in the business of restoring. And I believe He loves to put each of us on the Potter's wheel and give us a spin! Like a traffic "round about," that's the spin enabling us to take the correct exit and right our path once again.

God is emphatically capable of doing a miraculous and immediate restoration in you; however, He may choose not to. If He asks us to wait, it doesn't make His abilities untrue. That's our impatience! Upon numerous occasions, I've taken hard notice that things happen in God's time, not mine. He's never late and never early. He knows what He does in us will affect others. God is like the director of an orchestra, and we are the musicians. He understands everything we must do to have a harmonious life.

Your journey is a process. His help is on the way to restore you if you let him.

> We are hard pressed on every side, but not crushed; perplexed, but not in despair; persecuted, but not abandoned; struck down, but not destroyed (2 Corinthians 4:8-9 NIV).

> O house of Israel, can I not do with you as this potter? says the LORD. "Look, as the clay *is* in the potter's hand, so *are* you in My hand, O house of Israel!" (Jeremiah 18:6).

Chapter 2

Demolition Crew

Have you ever seen or watched a building being demolished? In all honesty, I've wanted to drive a big bulldozer or toss a wrecking ball into the side of a building and watch it crash! Sounds like something for my Bucket List. As I observe the dismantling of a building, it gives me a glimpse of what it's like to be totally undone by Christ so He can do a new thing in me. Try not to be too surprised that the messier things will become before the innovative can take place. Anyone who envisions shipshape order knows this when they tackle a task for the white-glove finish. In my house, I wonder where all that stuff came from and how it fit in one drawer or one shelf. Usually, I discover it wasn't all supposed to fit in there. That's the down side of "catchall" spaces; they get full.

On demolition sites, we see cement chunks, wire, dirt, rocks, wood, plastic, more wire, nails, brackets, and steel fixtures being separated respectively. It's the end of the building, but also a beginning of something new. Why do you think parts are being separated? Can't they be tossed in a landfill and covered up? Well, that's wrong on several levels. Most of the materials can be recycled and reused. Some parts will be significant for a new structure. Some, however, will be destroyed and never seen again. They will be burned, buried, or shipped into outer space. That's probably wrong also, but you get what I am saying. Everything has a measure of life in it, and not everything is used up when it appears to be expired.

Broken people are not absolute in such a state. Some are simply in need of rearranging, tweaking, or adjusting. God's people are not "throwaways." His Word says, He will refine us and test us. Let's look at the so-called dead parts. Now if something is buried, what can happen later in the natural elements? If it contains poisons, it can seep into the land, be carried distances with underground water flow, and cause illness and disease. It lacks any good thing to give life, and instead causes harm with its impurities.

How does this relate to us spiritually? If problems are covered up, there's always a chance they can resurface. That's a scary thought. Not recycling our emotions properly leaves to chance a costly reprocessing—that cost being precious lives.

Demolish the dead stuff in your life. Expect what God has in store by springing forth an exciting and brand new you. Savor what God is doing in your transformation.

> Therefore, if anyone is in Christ, he is a new creation; old things have passed away; behold, all things have become new (2 Corinthians 5:17).

> Then you shall drive out all the inhabitants of the land from before you, destroy all their engraved stones, destroy all their molded images, and demolish all their high places (Numbers 33:52).

> And no one puts new wine into old wineskins; or else the new wine bursts the wineskins, the wine is spilled, and the wineskins are ruined. But new wine must be put into new wineskins (Mark 2:22).

Chapter 3

Who Do You Agree With?

The awareness of who we've made an agreement with may be surprising. It could be our Enemy, Satan, who was cast down from heaven because he desired to usurp the authority of God. I can't imagine such a foolish idea. Jesus said, "I saw Satan fall like lightening from heaven" (Luke 10:18). God threw him out with a mighty force.

Our day-to-day life, trials, blessings, complacency, and distractions; all play out their roles. The visual for this message is imagining someone at our door. After pinpointing flaws and weaknesses, Satan knocks at our door with an enticing agenda of opportunities. Maybe you've heard the saying, "Looking at the world through rose-colored glasses." Well Satan is counting on that. Maybe having learned how to be on guard and aware of his deceitful tactics, we may not actually open the door. What he does, however, is leave the package anyway, placing it ever so gently like a treasure, rendering it as having merit.

Here's the thing, we're aware of our Enemy's modus operandi, but still we peek out the window preconceiving what might be awaiting our embrace. What's that old saying—"Curiosity killed the cat?" With a sigh, we ignore our better judgment as we watch him leave; but, there the package sits, looking lovely and tempting. We think about it some more. What should we do? Curiosity gets the best of us; we slowly open the door, approach timidly, and pick up the package. Why? We have continued to be mesmerized by its beauty and secret opportunity.

In reality, that package represents a marred future—the means to draw you off your purposeful path. We must take off the blinding rose-colored glasses and ask God to reveal any hidden agenda and schemes. Be watchful of your own eyes, and equip yourself with God's view.

I do not agree with you, Enemy of God, that I am going to have second best.

I do not agree that I am never going to have enough provision.

I do not agree with you!

I declare God is on my side, working in my life, and I will accept His best.

I do not agree that I'm going to lose my child to the world.
I do not agree that I will always be unhealthy.

Sometimes we simply need not answer the door.

> "Then Jesus said to him, 'Away with you, Satan! For it is written, "*You* shall worship the *LORD* your God, and Him only you shall serve" '" (Matthew 4:10).

> "But He turned and said to Peter, 'Get behind Me, Satan! You are an offense to Me, for you are not mindful of the things of God, but the things of men'" (Matthew 16:23).

> "Mark the blameless man, and observe the upright; for the future of that man is peace" (Psalm 37:37).

Chapter 4

Be of Sound Mind and Body

A healthy body plus healthy mind equals healthy relationships. Nourishing our body and mind is key to living well by exercising, communicating, and acquiring knowledge—all working together in unity. Our spiritual and physical selves cry out for sustenance. As we take care of our bodies, we must also take care of our spirit man. Cookies and milk are delicious, but a diet of this alone won't get the job done. We must digest a variety from the bounty God has provided us.

Equally important is what we feed our spirit. Media keeps us up to date on current events. Magazines and books can be entertaining or informing, and no doubt we enjoy them. These alone will not enhance or grow our spirit man. The Word strengthens our body and mind, which leads us to be in touch with Christ in all we do, see, and hear. The Holy Bible is the almanac of our lives.

Endeavoring to better care for ourselves, we can try probing the larger picture of everything connected to the other, causing functionality at the highest level. Certainly most of us ask for, pursue more, and expect challenges which motivate development. Surely, we want to be prepared for the answers to our prayers, along with the ability to handle responsibilities with trustworthiness. Possibly like some of you, I have a directory filled with items that get in the way of well-rounded fitness. Quite frankly, for most of them, I have to be the one to bring about the necessary modification by defining better options. Let's not beat ourselves up over what we haven't yet accomplished, but instead start each day with new hope. It's not always comfortable, but I have found that welcoming an accountability lifestyle is exactly what I should do. True friends, and yes, even spouses are good for this. They may open your eyes to where your starting point might be to move heaven and earth!

Honor Christ in all things. Doing so first with Him enhances our personal relationships, causing limitless coexistence. What He experienced on the cross deserves that we tend well to what He has given us.

Or do you not know that your body is the temple of the Holy Spirit *who is* in you, whom you have from God, and you are not your own? For you were bought at a price; therefore glorify God in your body and in your spirit, which are God's (1 Corinthians 6:19-20).

For no one ever hated his own flesh, but nourishes and cherishes it, just as the Lord *does* the church (Ephesians 5:29).

But I see a different law in the parts of my body, waging war against the law of my mind and taking me prisoner to the law of sin in the parts of my body (Romans 7:23 HCSB).

For those who are according to the flesh and are controlled by its unholy desires set their minds on and pursue those things which gratify the flesh, but those who are according to the Spirit and are controlled by the desires of the Spirit set their minds on and seek those things which gratify the [Holy] Spirit (Romans 8:5 AMPC).

Chapter 5

Pictures Are Worth a Thousand Emotions

Children grow up right before our eyes and enlarge our hearts to what feels like triple the size. The eyes and heart give us two distinct perspectives. The eye sees our world visually, and our heart sees through faith. When our son was born, we should have purchased stock in Kodak. Yes, we took that many pictures with actual film. There wasn't a camera in every phone back then. Almost daily, there are moments when I lovingly marvel and survey the many photographs in our home taken of our son. But, what stands out to me today is what I saw with my heart. In my faith during his earliest years, I caught only glimpses of what a blessing he would be to his dad and me. His aspiration to embrace life has been inspiring to us and those around him. That's beautiful to me, not perfect, but beautiful.

As parents, we love our children immeasurably. Even so, not nearly to the extent our heavenly Father does. We desire God's unsurpassed excellence for our children. He has entrusted us to be the best stewards of them we can possibly be. God desires us to lead lives of excellence and pass those ideals of decent morals and ethics on to our children. I used to think that leading an excellent life was unattainable. Not so. One's excellence means one's best. Excellence is not perfection. None of us will ever be perfect beings. That flawlessness is Christ himself—the One we ensue to be more like every day.

As parents, it's okay to take ourselves down off the meat hook and know that our parenting skills are limited and flawed. We're way too hard on ourselves sometimes. Find the joy on those ridiculous days we label as unsuccessful. Like any good inventor, it takes mistakes to discover what NOT to do. Progressing along our individual pathway, God has laid out incredible deeds to accomplish, if we choose Christ as our "standard," and not the world's. Tomorrow awaits us filled with what only faith can see today.

There is so much more than what we see with our natural eyes. Keep your dreams alive by engaging your faith.

Bind them on your fingers; Write them on the tablet of your heart (Proverbs 7:3).

"And he lifted his eyes and saw the women and children, and said, 'Who are these with you?' So he said, 'The children whom God has graciously given your servant'" (Genesis 33:5).

"And you, fathers, do not provoke your children to wrath, but bring them up in the training and admonition of the Lord" (Ephesians 6:4).

Chapter 6

Oh, the Joy of Parenting

The windows of opportunity for instilling virtue and character-building skills into our children are quite small, when we stop to think about it. I'm thankful my husband agreed with my desire to be a stay-at-home mom. Having our first and only child when I was 40 and my husband 50 caused us to prioritize for sure. I did not want to miss out on a single thing during this adventure; and I haven't.

In my job of domestic engineering, I've found that we mothers dedicate what we believe to be more than 24 hours a day to our families. I do my best to make every event or holiday one to remember. I'm the mom known to bake cookies at midnight for sleepovers or take kids to a 24-hour restaurant for a snack. I like to create new traditions, and nobody seems to mind how crazy they are. Creativity has no boundaries, and I live in the realm of eccentric, and that's ok.

I don't know why some people ask a stay-at-home mom, "What do you do all day? Don't you get bored?" The word *bored* was simply not allowed in our home; no time for that. My definition of the word *bored* was "NONSENSE!" Being a mom was and is the best job I've ever been awarded. The teaching possibilities are endless while mixed in with crazy and extreme fun. Ten years after moving to Tennessee, I received a wedding announcement from one of the girls that spent a lot of time at our home. She wrote a personal note to me that said she remembered the fun times at our home and that no one was allowed to say the word "bored!" Success!

I'm thankful for windows of opportunity. Our arms are open to our children, when they have hurt feelings, exaggerated ouches, and especially after we administer discipline. We lovingly laugh as we watch their joy of life, imagination, crazy drawings of us, and we especially like the tiny age-appropriate wisdom they absorb while learning. We dress them in their jammies sometimes for late nights at church (with only a few frowns from our church family) and enjoy dressing them daily the way **we** like. Then suddenly out of the blue, it's "Oh mom, I can't wear that." Sigh!

The number of children we have doesn't dictate the level of "tired"; we are on a scale of "one to scream." I had only one child and there were times my level of tired was off the charts. A cloud of weariness grips us all at one time or another, and all the good we try to accomplish seems to "go out the window." I have visualized a basket sitting outside one of my house windows. I imagine it to contain all those time-tested teachings that hypothetically went sailing through the window as if being sucked out by a hurricane. Imagine that basket sitting out in the open, full of many good and excellent things. It never fails; someone always takes notice of it. Get ready, because you are on the receiving end of a revelation here. It's called a blessing about your very own child. Soon you begin hearing about the kindness, honesty, and integrity displayed by your offspring. It's from a teacher, friend, another mom, or a complete stranger who affirms your energy and efforts that you consistently poured into your child was time well spent. You thought it was all for naught, as what you taught seemed to sail right out that window. God doesn't waste anything from our efforts.

Simply love through all things and all years with your children. God's Word says it's the greatest commandment. How powerful love is with such a great desire to survive.

> Behold, children *are* a heritage from the Lord, the fruit of the womb *is* a reward. Like arrows in the hand of a warrior, so *are* the children of one's youth. Happy *is* the man who has his quiver full of them; they shall not be ashamed, but shall speak with their enemies in the gate (Psalm 127:3-5).

> Let my teaching drop as the rain, My speech distill as the dew, as raindrops on the tender herb, and as showers on the grass (Deuteronomy 32:2).

Chapter 7

Creativity and Freedom

While driving my car, God dropped this thought into my lap—creativity and freedom. I keep a notebook handy as God seems to speak to me at the most odd and inconvenient times. I thought, *Lord, I appreciate what you've said, but please plant it in my heart for a later time of mulling it over because I AM driving.* Surely He's noticed the freeways these days! The truth is, God would like my ear inclined to Him at all times, whether I'm driving or at home sitting in my big comfy chair reading. I have been in conversation with someone when He plopped something mid-sentence into my mind. Then, there's the grocery store or the doctor's office, or the conversation you're having with someone you would rather not be having. . . and He speaks. That's praise! Saved by the voice of God! Anyway, I know to keep a notepad handy. How many weird places has He spoken to you? I suspect you will never forget what He said.

Creativity is freedom. You can't have creativity if you do not have the freedom to create. Don't you enjoy how they go hand-in-hand? When God speaks a Word, there are usually two things that happen: Hearing the Word, and then the action that follows. He begins revealing what He has given us. So in order for us to act upon His Word, He may have to make something known that's hidden in us. Don't stop when you hear a good word spoken! Do something amazing with it.

Now, this is where the Enemy of our soul steps in, because he doesn't want one bit of God's best revealed to us. He would rather pervert what God says, because he is the author of deception and operates fully within a hidden and downright sneaky agenda. Basically, he likes to trip us up by setting a trap, and then hope we will take the bait. Don't take the bait! If you happen to get your foot stuck in the trap and fall down, get back up and dust yourself off in pursuit of the action you need to take. A little dirt doesn't hurt anyone anyway. I don't know about you, but I appreciate those who are willing to get their hands dirty in order to glorify God. He never underestimates possibilities or what someone is capable of by what they look like. We have no idea what one person can accomplish when he/she gets in touch with the gifts God has given.

Ask God to reveal what you need to see so that you can fully act upon what it is while you seek direction. Fully utilize the freedom of creativity that you can have in Christ. Take your refuge in God, be original and generate something incredible. You just might be the person to show someone the WOW factor in his or her life.

> So that by two unchangeable things, in which it is impossible for God to lie, we who have fled for refuge might have strong encouragement to hold fast to the hope set before us (Hebrews 6:18 ESV).

> The proud have hidden a trap for me, and cords; they have spread a net by the wayside; they have set snares for me. Selah (Psalm 140:5 NASB).

> So he shepherded them according to the integrity of his heart, and guided them by the skillfulness of his hands (Psalm 78:72).

Chapter 8

The Arborist

A tree has seasons; so do people who must withstand constant change. Seasons of birth and death alike inspire new life. For example, the actual birth and death of humanity, as well as living the Christian life—as we die to our old selves, we are born again anew in Christ.

The tree is one of my favorite examples of how God revitalizes us. Our home in Brownsville, Oregon, was in the country and full of old-growth evergreen and maple trees. Their strength and immensity were a vision of irrefutable beauty in nature. The maple trees had leaves practically the size of table placemats! The fir trees held true to their name and were ever-green, no matter how bitter cold it was. The trees displayed their beauty in winter attire with heavily snow-laden branches bowing to the frozen ground below. One of our dearest friends likened our home to an oasis—a place of refreshing that welcomed many to have rest, no matter the weather.

As winter turned the corner to springtime, I would clip a few small branches from a maple tree. At this point, the soon-to-be leaves were only buds. Placing them in water, I sat them on my window sill, usually in the kitchen. By morning, I was amazed to see what transpired during the night. Leaves unfolded so quickly it seemed I could have watched the transformation. Springtime "springs" forth brilliantly because of the process of rest in winter.

One winter we experienced a severe and unusual storm. Due to horrific wind gusts, our largest maple tree toppled, leaving only a huge jagged stump. When the arborist finished trimming, he said it would more than likely die. Poor tree, it did look awful; but undeniably, my reply was, "Nope, it's going to live." Steadfast in my certainty, I noticed encircling the stump no less than a million branches within an incredibly short time! That's an exaggeration, of course, but there was a lot! Soon enough three larger main branches sprouted from the stump in the same place they used to be when the tree was full size in its glory days. Tiny shoots were popping out rapidly and thicker at the base. Though I definitely do not have a green thumb as my friends often remind me, I knew the sprouting of random branches would be a problem as to how nourishment was distributed to the tree. After all, I was believing for a tree again, not a bush. I trimmed as needed, promoting growth and strength to the main limbs. Before I knew it, there was a new and healthy maple tree taking form, as long as I maintained routine grooming.

We are like that tree, you and I. His Word removes dead things from our lives, so we can maintain new, healthy growth in promotion of His kingdom for as long as we live. Grow and prosper to the fullest and best God has for you.

> (As it is written, "*I have made you a father of many nations*") in the presence of Him whom he believed—God, who gives life to the dead and calls those things which do not exist as though they did (Romans 4:17).

> He shall be like a tree planted by the rivers of water, that brings forth its fruit in its season, whose leaf also shall not wither; and whatever he does shall prosper (Psalm 1:3).

Chapter 9

That Is So Irritating!

Bumble Bees, woodpeckers, barking dogs, and flower-eating deer are troublesome to me, and that's an understatement. The fish in my son's aquarium that I inherited have given me the nickname "Assassin." No matter how hard I try to take care of them they stop swimming. Seriously, it's irritating to me. The pet store people stopped letting me purchase anymore replacement fish. Who can understand these critters, and how can we live in harmony with them to make them stop barking, stop eating my flowers, stop pecking on my house, and stop making honey in my balcony?

The question is, what do we do when something irritates us? Do we get mad, offended, retaliate, or get even? Well, if our flesh reacts, that sounds about right. That method, however, garnered by experience, doesn't work with critters, because I've had countless battles with them while living in the country. In exasperation, the best I can do is ignore the irritant until I can find someone to fix the situation. The problem is, the more I try to ignore it, the more difficult, louder, and intense it becomes. Right?

One of the things the Bible says about animals, birds, insects, etc. is that we have dominion over them. I do understand what God means, but on a lighter note, I find it humorous because I don't speak Bumble Bee, bird, canine, fish, or deer to mention a few of my language barriers. It's a regular Tower of Babble.

What about when people irritate us with their diverse personalities, tone of voice, or quirkiness? Well, that requires a good deal more skill and refinement. Working things out with some people makes dealing with animals a walk in the park. The truth is, I find myself irritating at times, and I'm sure others do too! Even my husband has said to me, "I don't understand you," and I know I have definitely gotten on his nerves. I can't possibly be the only one with this truthful confession. Again, it doesn't help if I get upset, angry, or go for revenge if annoyed by someone. The effect is about the same as with animals—it doesn't work. Pertaining to people though, if I react badly, it makes me feel worse, and I also feel foolish, mean, and disrespectful. Then, regret sets in because these are my brothers and sisters in Christ. I do not have dominion over them like I do the animal kingdom. Let's try every day to live in harmony with others in our lives.

Find the gift of forbearance within you, and His way will always break any language barrier that may exist.

> For you shall have a covenant with the stones of the field, and the beasts of the field shall be at peace with you (Job 5:23).

> If it is possible, as much as it depends on you, live peaceably with all men (Romans 12:18).

Chapter 10

You're Made the Way You're Made

Not every morning is the same for us, is it? I wake up, usually feeling on top of the world. Usually. The days I don't are kind of sluggish, and nothing seems to be as it should be. I may not be able to put my finger on exactly what's wrong, but one thing I do know—it isn't right. Sooner than later, I try to get a correct perspective so my day will take on a pioneering spirit—one that looks forward to what I would otherwise miss. Each of us is uniquely made with purpose, no matter how we think we feel at any particular time. In the Bible, David praised God because he knew he was fearfully and wonderfully made.

We are exquisite in the eyes of our Creator. For some, it is difficult to think this way as we guard against being prideful. But this is not about pride. It's about our unique gifts, personalities, and characteristics that make us distinctive. It is how we are separate, yet connected to bring out the best in each other. When we view others as gifted in their respective ways, we complement one another. We become extraordinary for God's kingdom.

We can do many things to improve our areas of weakness, but we must not forget to focus on our areas of strength. If we spend too much time trying to improve in areas just to be like someone else, it's highly possible that our unique qualities will become stagnant. Instead of thinking about wanting to be like someone else, perhaps you should give some thought to how many people want to be like you. It works both ways.

We can't let envy or jealousy keep us from appreciating how someone else shines. We have our own glimmer that radiates and penetrates a darkened world. Sprinkle some bling! When you look in the mirror, what do you see? No matter what your answer is, ask God to show you what He sees. We are made in His image.

> There is a splendor of the sun, another of the moon, and another of the stars; for one star differs from another star in splendor (1 Corinthians 15:41 HCSB).

For just as each of us has one body with many members, and these members do not all have the same function, so in Christ we though many, form one body, and each member belongs to all the others. We have different gifts, according to the grace given to each of us. If your gift is prophesying, then prophesy in accordance with your faith; If it is serving, then serve, if it is teaching, then teach; if it is to encourage, then give encouragement; if it is giving then give generously; if it is to lead, do it diligently; if it is to show mercy, do it cheerfully (Romans 12:4-8 NIV).

Then David danced before the LORD with all *his* might; and David *was* wearing a linen ephod (2 Samuel 6:14).

Chapter 11

Adornment

When we worship the Lord, we are, in a sense, decorating ourselves with an enrichment of praise that honors Him with adoration. This takes place within us and is so deeply rooted that we cannot help but demonstrate His presence outwardly. Jewelry, on the other hand, is displayed on the outside of us as ornamental to enhance our appearance. It is displayed in its entirety, and there is nothing more to it.

What are we wearing in the spirit to represent and glorify God? Are we embracing goodness that shows honor and, when released, brings liberation to others? If we could observe our reflection in a sanctified mirror, we would see a different reflection from what our natural eye sees. When it comes to ministering to women, this is a worthy area into which we should speak life. All the exposure to the world's standards can be hurtful. We ask, "Do I measure up?" Maybe the better question would be to ask ourselves, *"By which standards are we trying to measure ourselves?"*

When I was a little girl, my friends and I played dress-up and were told how beautiful we looked. It was fun during youthful innocence. Much transitioning goes on between this stage and maturity. As we develop, it's not uncommon to compare ourselves with others to such a degree it may cause us to become unhealthy in the way we think and view ourselves.

I personally don't believe there is anything wrong at all with children playing dress-up and putting on play makeup. As mature women, we may desire to wear our Sunday best and apply makeup to enhance our unique features. I say make the best of what God has given each of us. In my world, you will see me looking a variety of ways! Some of them better than others, but hopefully I am the same person.

However, along the way, I think the word "beautiful" should blossom into what the deeper meaning really is. Beauty is a reflection of a healthier life. It's a life that exudes wellness and is accented with the fruit of the Spirit, which reaches out to others and welcomes others to us.

One of my prayers goes something like this:

Lord, we adore You and want to adorn ourselves with the fruit of the Spirit. Life is not perfect and never will be until we move into our final home of eternity with You. We thank You for grace, both when needing it and extending it to others. We don't accept lies that harm us. Reveal wrong thinking and teach us Your standards. Uproot weeds that strangle, and plant seeds of Your truth. When a kind word is thought, let it be spoken. Hearts are yearning and longing for something, and that something is You. Use women to encourage, appreciate, and uplift one another. Speak words of encouragement to children and women of all ages. Amen.

Then adorn yourself *with* majesty and splendor, and array yourself with glory and beauty (Job 40:10).

But the fruit of the Spirit is love, joy, peace, longsuffering, kindness, goodness, faithfulness, gentleness, self-control. Against such there is no law (Galatians 5:22-23).

Chapter 12

The Resistance

Suddenly and exactly when we need it, God reveals a word to us, like manna from heaven! This is done abruptly, in my opinion, because He doesn't want to give us a chance to dissect and deplete it to nothing more than hearsay. Also, I don't think He wants to listen to all the excuses we can muster up. Our opposition is better aimed at principalities and powers, than that of challenging God.

I am encouraged by reading what David did in 1 Samuel 17:48. He hurried and ran toward his opposition. That's a strong precedent to follow. Stir up trust and faith for what God says you can do, because He has prepared the way and will meet you there. We can all lead victorious lives. Don't be afraid to take aim and commit yourself to a challenge, because there is a will of iron in you.

The thing about resistance is the authority it has. Someone can simply stand still and be stalwart against an element opposing them. There won't be a lot of thrashing about, because we are stern and well braced against what we are facing. The more we find ourselves resisting, the closer it must be to us. That is a scary thought! Discernment is crucial to what and how our opposition operates. I believe each of us has untapped strength when push comes to shove.

Our physical and spiritual resistance is complimentary to one another. As we take thoughts captive, our ability to recognize the subtle schemes of the Enemy becomes real. At that, we plant our feet, stand ready, fully armed, strong, and powerful in the Spirit. Again, the exercise of resistance fortifies our physical and spiritual selves. God unifies both forces to empower us, contrary to that which is bent on destroying us.

We submit to God's authority and no other. What He has for us is designed and set apart purposely for such a time as this.

> For we do not wrestle against flesh and blood, but against principalities, against powers, against the rulers of the

darkness of this age, against spiritual hosts of wickedness in the heavenly places (Ephesians 6:12).

Therefore submit to God. Resist the devil and he will flee from you (James 4:7).

We demolish arguments and every pretension that sets itself up against the knowledge of God, and we take captive every thought to make it obedient to Christ (2 Corinthians 10:5 NIVUK).

He will not allow your foot to be moved; He who keeps you will not slumber (Psalm 121:3).

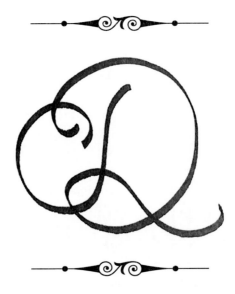

Chapter 13

Why Bless God?

A particular thought came to me the other day that maybe people don't understand what it means to "bless God." Why should we? He has everything; what could we possibly do that would bless Him? Several ways come to mind: how we treat His other children, how we reverence Him, and how we appreciate him. How about this concept? We love Him for who He is, not what He can do for us. We are not to set ourselves above others as though they are not worthy of dignity and respect. From the people we acknowledge as lifelong family or friends to the person we meet by chance, they are all God's sons and daughters. He is our creator, and He fashioned us to love and care for others always.

Parents are pleased with their children during all stages of growth—from babies to well beyond adulthood. As parents, my husband and I didn't withhold blessing our son, even when we were displeased with his behavior. There was a broad spectrum of mentorship, which included correction as needed. What we were watching for was development in all areas of maturing. We could not possibly consider waiting to do things with him or for him until he was perfect. I don't know anyone on this planet that could or should ever hold to that criterion.

Explore all opportunities consistently coming our way, leading our children to the enlightenment and pursuit of correct behavior. Whether it's displayed among friends, acquaintances, team members, church family, or strangers; behavior blesses God. His acceptance and love for us is unchanging and unconditional through any circumstance. We must, however, understand that accountability for our behavior is necessary in order to receive what is paramount for all our days. No one is more capable of meeting us right where we are than our heavenly Father. Aren't you glad that He loves us so much that He will not withhold blessings while we continually mature? Consequently, what we sow into the Kingdom matters.

Godliness is the connection between God and man. It is not a term that means comparison with God. We could not begin to touch His invincible sovereignty, because He is omnipotent, but we are not. As we delve more deeply into what Godliness is, we see a relevancy to minister to ourselves. I suppose most people do not think of it as something we do for ourselves, but do only for others. Consider it though; if we implemented a salt-of-the-earth mindset ministering to ourselves, it would certainly make a difference in relationship.

> Only take heed to yourself, and diligently keep yourself, lest you forget the things your eyes have seen, and lest they depart from your heart all the days of your life. And teach them to your children and your grandchildren (Deuteronomy 4:9).

> For I say, through the grace given to me, to everyone who is among you, not to think *of himself* more highly than he ought to think, but to think soberly, as God has dealt to each one a measure of faith (Romans 12:3).

> Bless the LORD, all his works, in all places of his dominion. Bless the LORD, O my soul! (Psalm 103:22).

Chapter 14

Prayer Is Serious Business

How, when, where, and why is prayer important? ALWAYS AND ANYWHERE! Prayer affects circumstances in us and our surroundings. Prayer is an amazing instrument; it can set and change the atmosphere. Imagine how that action revolutionizes circumstances! However you pray, just PRAY! Don't worry how you sound or what you look like.

Have you ever shared a need with someone, and they replied, "I will pray for you?" After you part ways, do you ever wonder if they actually prayed for you? I'm incapable of actually knowing the statistics of this question. However, what I can share with you is, there have been times I told someone I would pray for them, and I did not. I received God's conviction with my head hanging down, as I was stirred to compassion. Prayer is indeed serious business, and I do my best to keep my word to pray for a need, even if it's unconventional in place and time. I don't like drawing attention to private conversation, but I can usually find a way for that person to know a "breath prayer" has gone to the throne of the Father before we part ways.

A breath prayer is also known as the "Jesus Prayer," or "Prayer of the Heart." I have often introduced this to the daughters I mentor. Some have recently begun to invest in their prayer life, while others pray more easily than some. A breath prayer can be spoken with the rhythm of your breath. By memorizing several scriptures one is particularly fond of and shortening them to a few words, is a quick way to call on them when needed. We should never doubt that our prayers are heard from the simple ones to the radical.

Your speech need not be specifically eloquent, precise, politically correct, loud, or soft. More important, your desire increases to present all things before the throne of God. He knows everything already, and it's useless to hide anything from Him. Depending upon what needs have touched your heart is what determines your scope of prayer. A broken favorite pencil compared to a loved one having open heart surgery will move you to pray accordingly. Being sensitive to the Holy Spirit indeed helps when you don't know how to pray.

When prayerfully seeking answers, using the Bible surpasses all other references. The Holy Bible in its entirety contains the irrefutable living Word for your course of action. Taking the Word out of context to find the answer **we want** can lead to reckless implementation, and the results can be disastrous. I use the 20/20 system. Reading 20 verses, which come before a scripture and 20 verses after the same scripture gives greater understanding and imparts wisdom from God.

Prayer deepens our relationships and prayer should never be underestimated.

> Likewise the Spirit also helps in our weaknesses. For we do not know what we should pray for as we ought, but the Spirit Himself makes intercession for us with groanings which cannot be uttered (Romans 8:26).

> Pray without ceasing (1 Thessalonians 5:17).

Chapter 15

I Don't Need Discipline; I'm Always Right

Once we have knowledge, we have responsibility. With responsibility we need accountability. Consequences then are a reflection of how accountable we have been. So this is the formula: knowledge + responsibility + accountability = consequences, or what I like to call the "fruit" in our lives.

Brothers and sisters spanning all generations have not always lived by this formula. Youth of today are the church of the future. It is essential we consider it our duty to be "real" with them in articulating the Word of God. Decisions will vary about the conditions of how and where we arrive at any particular location. Many times we ask, "How in the world did I get here?" Reflecting on what the difference is between living "in the world" and living "of the world" will show why none of us are exempt from this observation.

Plenty of people are watching us while our lives are in plain view like a department store window display. We continue to work on the formula that assists us to be at our best, as in apprenticeship. First and foremost, instruction should be complete, not only when something is right or wrong, but also understanding why the precepts are right or wrong. We can't leave out the "why" and simply say "because" or "do what I say, not what I do." It's not in the best interest of anyone to adhere only to parts of the Bible. That's like leaving out part of a map and expecting to arrive safely to a destination . . . or arrive at all.

Living an active Bible life is not life on "easy street," and strong teachings are never an easy pill to swallow. A few deficient responses from someone who has received godly correction might be: "I find that very offensive"; "Well!! I've never heard of such a thing"; or "I thought you really cared about me." All the while, truth says: "The shoe fits, and you should listen to correction from godly people because they do care." We can always share our reference material.

The challenge here is to admit and accept the fact we could possibly be wrong. Walk in humility and say thank you for telling me the whole truth. To me, true humility is when I believe I'm 100 percent correct, yet acknowledge the fact that I could still somehow be wrong. If we think we are always right, we will remain on the merry-go-round and never see what's beyond the same old circle.

Our lives have a myriad of junctures. Each one prepares us for the next. When coming to a fork in the road, consider the sequel that will follow your choice. With great humility, embrace, teach, and release people of all ages to walk out of a church building and **be** the church.

> Blessed is the one you discipline, Lord, the one you teach from your law (Psalm 94:12 NIV).

> The fear of the Lord is the beginning of knowledge, but fools despise wisdom and instruction (Proverbs 1:7).

> As many as I love, I rebuke and chasten: be zealous therefore, and repent (Revelation 3:19 KJV).

Chapter 16

Craving You, Lord, Is Fleeting; Greater That I Desire You

When we have desire, it's mostly for something we perceive as beneficial. Passion is stirred in us to be in pursuit at any cost. Nothing can divert us, and we turn a deaf ear to anyone who tries to get us to do otherwise. I hope I am always stirred by a worthy cause that draws others to awareness, so there will be a joining of hands to victory. We must be about something and make a difference to the quality of our lives and the lives of others. I believe when we seek truth, it's more than a sweep across the landscape with our eyes to hopefully get a glimpse of what we desire. When I seek, I mean to take apart the landscape bit by bit to discover what I cannot be without. The Word tells us when we seek, we will find.

But let's think outside the box for a moment. Can you imagine having a desire for bad things? That's difficult to do, because I don't knowingly want to desire unpleasant things at all and I'm unaware of anyone who does. But if I'm walking in unawareness of the difference between what's good for me and what's not, I'm certainly not in line with what's going to be God's best. Simply put, I am on the wrong track. My pilgrimage is to become a better person day by day. The Word tells us we are to desire the heart of God. This means His very best and nothing less.

There are times when I ask myself if I am only craving a relationship with God. I welcome those checkpoints for self-evaluation. Craving is a temporary want that will soon diminish. When I'm craving something sweet to eat, my flesh won't shut up until the craving is satisfied! When I desire something, it's from a deeper place and a quick fix won't be satisfying or eternal. How vested am I in travailing for what I know is most excellent for me and will turn my craving into desire?

Relationships between Christ and His people are kindled like a fire. There is an igniting that may only be a craving at first, but then it intensifies to a yearning that is completely consuming. You might say that craving exists on the outside of us—our flesh—and that can change like the weather. Desire is lasting and lives in the deepest recesses of our hearts and minds.

Heavenly eternity is worth being sought after, and I pray that I will never allow that flame to expire.

> Lord, the God of our fathers Abraham, Isaac and Israel, keep these desires and thoughts in the hearts of your people forever, and keep their hearts loyal to you (1 Chronicles 29:18 NIV).

> Rather, clothe yourselves with the Lord Jesus Christ, and do not think about how to gratify the desires of the flesh (Romans 13:14 NIV).

> O Lord, I pray, please let Your ear be attentive to the prayer of Your servant, and to the prayer of Your servants who desire to fear Your name; and let Your servant prosper this day, I pray, and grant him mercy in the sight of this man. For I was the king's cupbearer (Nehemiah 1:11).

Chapter 17

No Such Thing as Buying More Time

If you're like me, at one point or another you've wanted to somehow acquire more time. That's not likely to happen, because God has set in place a 24-hour-per-day schedule, no more, no less. It's wishful thinking to imagine a store where we could literally purchase more of such a valuable commodity. If there were such a place, it would more likely further my dilemma of not having enough hours in a day. I would find an increase of unfinished tasks by receiving more time on the clock along with false expectations of being able to accomplish more, not to mention, up to my eyeballs in debt to the "time store."

In my city, we have businesses on just about every corner where you can basically buy more cash. You sign excitedly on the dotted line, get the cash right away, but the cost is more than you anticipated in the end. There are many programs to help us pay back debt, but there's no way to pay back time. It's gone forever.

The best we can hope for is to manage what we have. Take a summary of current work, church, and community projects, as well as family needs. It's possible for some of us to be quickly convicted here, because we're already aware of the value that's been assigned in some areas before even beginning to itemize. Assign each of them a value from zero being the lowest in priority, to 10 being the highest, then you're ready to prioritize. Now consider the allotted 24 hours per day, seven days per week, four weeks per month, and the 12 months per year that God has amply given you. How does everything add up? Do you have a lot of tens? If so, it's time to consider reprioritizing. Remember to have a good attitude, because we don't want to get tripped up. Our goal is to be liberated.

The next question is, "Can you say no?" Actually, the way I see it is someone that can say no is able to accomplish a great deal more than one who can't. I have a precious friend who says yes to everything. His life is filled with unresolved issues and incomplete undertakings. But if you want a yes answer he is the one to "go to." I must say he means well, has a right heart, and I appreciate how he is gifted in kindness. However, a yes answer without follow through has basically zero effect. Some people are capable of numerous activities and doing them well. I do not fall into this category, and I am okay with that because I understand everyone is gifted in his or her own way to shine.

God has taken the universal language of numbers and applied spiritual value. He can help you do all things that He authors.

> There is a time for everything, and a season for every activity under the heavens (Ecclesiastes 3:1 NIV).

> He who keeps his command will experience nothing harmful; and a wise man's heart discerns both time and judgment (Ecclesiastes 8:5).

Chapter 18

What's on Your Schedule Today?

Spending time with God does not necessarily need to be planned. If that were the case, we would miss opportunity after opportunity to be in His presence. Do you think He's unable to keep up with your schedule? He's always right there with you, ready to chat or have a deep discussion. A better way to think about this is that God is *omnipresent*—He is everywhere at the same time. Consider the following: You never have to wait for Him, He can always hear you even in a whisper, and He is your safe place to speak your mind. Remember to listen though. We can trust Him even if we don't understand fully. A portion at a time is how He made us to operate. Busy parents, work schedules, traffic jams, stalled engines, flat tires, long lines at the grocery or hardware store, sick children, planning a party, mending feelings, ending a relationship, finding lost keys, getting married, preparing a speech, walking at the park, moving, cleaning, yard work, dealing with enemies, playing with your kids, getting fired; the list goes on and on. He's there with you.

Years ago I wrestled with the scripture about what it meant to pray without ceasing. If I did that, how would I get anything else done? Years of trial and error led to enlightenment. It means to include God in every aspect of my daily life, like having a best friend with me 24 hours a day with whom I can share anything. Actually, He's better than a best friend. I like to share most everything with my husband, and trust me; he tells me there are some things which he passes the buck to God Almighty. This is where that phrase in our wedding vows—"for better or for worse"—comes in handy. I'm glad God is okay with getting the "worst" of me.

One of the things I repeatedly thought was that my prayers might be insignificant and God didn't have time for them. He listens like we are the only one speaking and that there is nothing more important than what we are saying. Another fallacy was that I didn't think I could keep praying for the same thing; for example, "praying through about a situation." Just like we have to repeat something to memorize it; we can speak to Him about an ongoing situation until it is resolved in one way or another. In some state of affairs, we pray out of obedience until we can pray from the heart. Prayer is a process of relating. It's building relationship and creating a bond with the One who holds all answers in all matters.

God has given us many gifts, and one of them is spontaneity. Like a cat that suddenly decides to be in another room. If you like cats, you know what I mean. Just like that and in an instant, you can pray. It doesn't matter when or where you speak to Him; He only cares that you do. Even though He knows everything, I think it means more to Him when we tell Him what we need to say.

> Pray without ceasing, in everything give thanks; for this is the will of God in Christ Jesus for you (1 Thessalonians 5:17-18).

> And whatever things you ask in prayer, believing, you will receive (Matthew 21:22).

Chapter 19

Who We Are and Who We Are Not

God's desire for us is to be His, and He wants us no matter what our condition is. There's no point in fretting, simply trust that whatever reflection you see of yourself or how you think others see you, know that God still wants you. Potential is what God sees because His view of us is through the eyes of His Son, Jesus. We can welcome and embrace direction as we display our complete person to Him. That's like laying it all out on a table within plain view. We develop feelings of defenselessness and vulnerability also, because like an X-ray machine, our entire being is seen with clarity. It may be difficult to do, but immediately a light shines on what is exposed. All of us are in need of change, and this method is effective to bring it about. God never puts us in a defenseless state, but rather His Word, which enables us.

When I go to the altar and pray, I practice leaving my burdens there. Just as important, I remember to make an exchange with God. That means I do not leave the altar without taking His promises with me. I take everything I like about myself and everything I don't, all I want to be and all that I am not. I also embrace this act of worship for the sake of others I am praying for. I bring anger, resentment, obligations, worry, sin, disability, mistakes, agendas, needs, praise, tears, burdens, comparisons, jealousy, pride, temptation, failure, hatred, judgment of myself and others, weakness, expectations, sickness, struggle, secrets, guilt, debt, debtor, disappointment, reasoning, misunderstandings, confusion, criticism, doubt, pain, fear, disgust, discrepancy, dilemma, fault, resentment, motives, unforgiveness, offenses, and the offenses from the person who offended me. That's a long list! Might I suggest you organize your own personal list and begin making an exchange with God?

Also, I bring joy, love, refreshing, kindness, companionship, delight, gifts, hope, commitment, pursuits, heart for revelation, relationship, willingness, ability, dreams, gratefulness, assignments, adventure, mission, strengths, family, friends, and the stranger I met today. Bring your history and your future, every path you have traveled and the one you're on right now, citizenship, leaders of our country, and the seats they will occupy, realms of authority, programs, every unanswered prayer, thoughts, and questions. Bring the "stuff" you don't even know why you keep. Unravel your cares, and be completely "undone" at the altar! This is a long list also and that's because God's promises are many.

Bring every color of gladness you have experienced and every depth of sadness you have known. Lay everything at the altar, and experience Christ's comfort and the "oil of joy" in exchange "for mourning."

> Come to Me, all *you* who labor and are heavy laden, and I will give you rest (Matthew 11:28).

> The LORD is near to the brokenhearted and saves the crushed in spirit (Psalm 34:18 ESV).

> Therefore everyone who hears these words of mine and puts them into practice is like a wise man who built his house on the rock (Matthew 7:24 NIV).

Chapter 20

What Do Your Words Actually Say?

Most everyone has to lead for a time in some kind of capacity. Whether I'm conversing with someone, writing, mentoring, preparing notes, or in the act of critiquing or correcting, I would like the information I have in my possession to be factual and reliable. Also, I appreciate that what's being said to me is trustworthy, since I'm going to respond, make decisions, and answer questions based on accuracy. If I need to relay information, it's important that it's worthy of being passed on. If precision is lacking, then reports, mentoring, teaching, or correcting become misinterpreted. Also, with accurate information, I'm able to convey a message in a beneficial way. I can't think of a place under the sun where this method would not lead to a positive outcome.

Just as truth matters, so does the way we address others and the tone of voice we use. That's a hard one to recognize, because we don't hear how we sound to others in the same way that they hear us. My husband is a sincere monitor of this, and I need reminding of it frequently. It's helpful, if I stop and think before I respond. He says I'm as subtle as a train wreck! Yikes! That can be bad, so my tone of voice is a constant challenge for me. All I can say is, I'm not where I need to be, but thank God, I'm not where I used to be. One of the most constructive helps I practice is to take my thoughts captive before I speak, as it says in the Bible. It awards me better communication. Try it.

Are there times you go on and on about something that should no longer have your words applied to it? Humbly, I admit having an excessive tendency toward that bad habit. This has especially been a problem when I have tried to add to or outdo what the Holy Spirit has already done in a superlative manner. Let me say it this way: I believe God has already addressed whatever my words were failing to convey. If the Holy Spirit's conviction has impressed upon someone's lack of judgment or error, there's no need for me to add a thing to it. I could not begin to do a better job, and at that point I am interfering.

Gather up God's Word and initiate teaching moments for others when appropriate, and don't forget to allow the benefit of said words to fall upon your own ears. It's constructive to embark on an approach of remedy and restoration through all situations. My words must be pure and not tainted with my own sins. Also, we must be a reflection of Christ, by speaking in ways that can be heard as inspirational toward excellence.

My lips will not speak wickedness, nor my tongue utter deceit (Job 27:4).

Having shod your feet with the preparation of the gospel of peace (Ephesians 6:15).

For the Holy Spirit will teach you in that very hour what you ought to say (Luke 12:12).

Chapter 21

I Will Not Be Moved

Without the foundational strength of a root system, trees would undoubtedly topple revealing their weakness to remain allegiant. Roots act as an anchor that gives them steadiness. Some root cores are wide, some deep and some are both. Which system depends greatly upon what's happening above ground, like what kind of terrain it is and weather conditions of an area. Much goes on underground to take care of what goes on above! Probably one of the most determining factors is wind. The interesting thing about wind is you can't see it, but you can sure see the effect it has.

I had a personal experience about the effect of wind. Our home in Brownsville, Oregon, encountered a freak storm one year. We lived atop a hill, and the mountain sides that surrounded our home were covered with trees. If there were gusts below us, all those trees buffered us to such a degree we were usually unaware of any high winds. Then as progress would have it, the property down the backside of ours was logged which made a huge difference in how our trees withstood storms. Though the trees on our property were quite aged, most of them developed only shallow root systems, apparently. Had they experienced windy conditions on a more regular basis, they would have probably developed stronger and deeper roots.

During this crazy storm, I looked out my window and saw the ground surrounding one of our enormous fir trees moving like the swell of ocean waves! Imagine that for a moment. I certainly will never forget that sight. My husband had told me earlier, "Go down to the family room because most of that area is underground." Unfortunately, I did not do that. My curiosity got the best of me, and I was remiss of rational thinking. I was fixated on investigating outside. Bad idea! Not only did I look outside, but I also ventured out and was smacked on the head by a rather large and rapidly traveling branch. Fifteen stitches later, I would be fine. In the end, we lost 23 trees, and some of them fell within inches of touching our home. We were thankful, because it could have been worse. The upside is we had an increase of firewood to cut for winter. If I hadn't gone out in the wind, I could have avoided the accident I had; the result of horrific wind effects.

What's going on within you and around you that's affecting your ability to stand firm? As children of God, are we strengthening our spiritual root system? What's weakening you and could potentially cause you to fall? Are we nourishing and equipping our minds so we can see, speak, hear God's direction, and have clarity and understanding? We must cultivate ourselves with living water that feeds our soul. We can become as strong as tempered steel, and at the same time, be able to bend like a willow. Strength needs to reside with flexibility so we do not collapse. We serve a mighty God who can take our mistakes and use them for good.

> He took also of the seed of the land, and planted it in a fruitful field; he placed it by great waters, and set it as a willow tree. And it grew, and became a spreading vine of low stature, whose branches turned toward him, and the roots thereof were under him: so it became a vine, and brought forth branches, and shot forth sprigs (Ezekiel 17:5-6 KJV).

> And men of all nations, from all the kings of the earth who had heard of his wisdom, came to hear the wisdom of Solomon (1 Kings 4:34).

Chapter 22

Unexpected Surprise

We can't plan on the unexpected, but we can be wisdom- and discernment-ready when it comes. Easier said than done, right? What's involved in the unexpected is absolutely anything and everything—the unimaginable! It usually comes when you haven't even had time to throw an anchor overboard like you would on a boat to stabilize yourself. Your attempts to get a grip and remain steadfast are obliterated by a slew of absurd and unreasonable thoughts. You are completely caught off guard. We don't have time to look for who's to blame; we have to act.

With the blessing of children in our lives, we must expect the unexpected. The truth of the matter is life does not happen without unplanned upsets. The most we can do is prepare as best we can each day. This doesn't mean we understand it. It means we have to deal with it, whether we want to or not, in the best way possible. When it comes to children, we can't just say, "Well, I wasn't expecting that; therefore, I don't have to acknowledge it." That's humorous at best. This is one of my favorite times to ask: "Okay, God, what do you want me to get out of this? It's going to take me some time to find a remedy for this situation, and I would like not to be empty-handed for next time."

Our children in all their glory can be illusory beings. Sometimes, we don't even know what spaceship they got off. And there are even a few times I wanted to get my child to Cape Canaveral in time to get him aboard for his return lift-off to where I imagined he was from. Realistically, our children probably think the same of us more than we would like to admit.

As parents, we are entrusted with their preciousness and upbringing to the best of our limited abilities. Yes, God has entrusted them to our stewardship. I'm happy to say parent/child relationships never end. They evolve into the phenomenal relationships also known as a miracle. We strive to give them healthy independence within God's boundaries. Wonderfully, His borders allow for mistakes, growing, learning, questioning, and individualism that develop character and personality. Their unique gifts unfold as they embrace life. So when they do weird things; stop, take a moment, and remember you were in their shoes at one time. Trust me; they will one day be in yours.

> Therefore, preparing your minds for action, and being sober-minded, set your hope fully on the grace that will be brought to you at the revelation of Jesus Christ (1 Peter 1:13 ESV).

> Preach the word; be ready in season *and* out of season; reprove, rebuke, exhort, with great patience and instruction (2 Timothy 4:2 NASB).

> Therefore you also be ready, for the Son of Man is coming at an hour you do not expect (Matthew 24:44).

Chapter 23

People Watchers

Do you ever sit in a judgment seat and exhibit flawed intentions? If you do, it's usually a combination of a situation and people. It is good to understand how this type of inspection is demonstrated in God's Word. Wisdom tells us to take a look inwardly and see if a finger should be pointed in our own direction. Basically, it serves us well to "red flag" ourselves firsthand. The scrutiny I am speaking about is what comes from jealousy, envy, bitterness, resentment, and the like. One of the roots of this kind of thinking is comparison. That's when our thoughts get twisted and we feast on thoughts that are deceiving. If we weren't comparing ourselves to someone else, this kind of evaluation probably would not rise up in us. How fantastic if we could live in 100 percent harmony and appreciation of each other's distinctiveness.

In our eyes, when people fail us, we must understand that the Enemy always uses people to hurt others. This happens among all relationships—spouses, children, entire families, the workplace, church, and strangers. Interestingly, we experience false comfort when we view strangers with an irrelevant attitude and eye. On this topic, I've observed where assessment and evaluation walk without discernment. It's the "sight-seeing" business called people watching. For example, we sit with a friend at a restaurant or mall and have a comment of slight about everyone we see on the runway of fashion. Remember that, the next time you're at the mall or walking by a restaurant window. Oh yes! I am speaking to myself as well!

Here's the deal; I learned how to do this very thing from my mom! She enjoyed people watching. I don't think she meant any harm at all, but she was quite critical at times. There were times her nitpicking words were addressed to me and my generation. Criticism weighs a great deal when we have it thrust upon us. There were gaps in mine and my mom's communication, and I recognize my stubbornness and strong will played a big part.

People change by different degrees, depending on their ability. I finally recognized there were ways in my mom that were never going to change, no matter how much I wanted them to be different. What I understood to a greater degree was that I could change myself. In doing so, I was free to love her in spite of what agitated me. My perception of how she really did love me transitioned also. As my walk with Christ became more passionate, I endeavored to know her on a deeper level. I took into account how she was raised, how she learned to communicate, who taught her, and what she wasn't taught. With respect and a loving way, this beautiful journey with my mom had a promising outcome on her life and mine. We often-times misunderstand what we don't understand. Who am I to judge some-one's best?

> And besides they learn *to be* idle, wandering about from house to house, and not only idle but also gossips and busybodies, saying things which they ought not (1 Timothy 5:13).

> Let no corrupt word proceed out of your mouth, but what is good for necessary edification, that it may impart grace to the hearers (Ephesians 4:29).

Chapter 24

I Have a Stomachache

You don't feel sick, anxious, worried, mad, hungry, afraid, nervous, or apprehensive, yet, there is an ache. It seems to keep you from focusing on much of anything and you're unable to sort through what it might be. Your mind is abuzz with a plethora of thoughts. At this point, the power of temptation promotes erroneous thinking. Why is it that fearful thoughts hit us so hard with the unknown? I know people who turn to the Internet first thing and research whatever is ailing them. Then, they wish they had never done so, because now it causes them to feel worse than they imagined. It isn't true, of course, but they have read all the worst-case scenarios. Thoughts begin to gravitate toward unhealthy affiliation.

Why don't we think positive thoughts immediately? The Bible tells us it isn't our nature. We have to choose goodness. He has given us authority, but we don't often take specific authority over our mind and thoughts like we should. Christ tells us to put into practice correct thinking. Go to God in prayer instead of the Internet. It's the best way to keep the Enemy from hacking into your mind.

The thing about this ache is it hasn't anything to do with an ailment, but it can become one if not treated correctly. The ache I am talking about here comes from deep within your belly; the kind of ache that doesn't fit into any other category. For my female friends, you know exactly what I am talking about if you have given birth. With my first and only childbirth, the nurse asked me if I felt like I was ready to push. I said with great conviction "I have no idea!" Then suddenly I did know.

The analogy is God wants to birth something in all of us, and He is stirring you to bring forth the very thing He has placed within you. What have you been dreaming or what causes you to be stirred to passion for His kingdom? The pain is what gets your attention that something is about to happen! The discomfort will be well worth it.

> And whatever you do, do it heartily, as to the Lord and not
> to men (Colossians 3:23).

With Your hand from men, O LORD, from men of the world who have their portion in this life, and whose belly You fill with Your hidden treasure. They are satisfied with children, and leave the rest of their possession for their babes (Psalm 17:14).

When the righteous are in authority, the people rejoice; But when a wicked man rules, the people groan (Proverbs 29:2).

Chapter 25

Catapult Yourself for God

Once you're out in the deep for God, then you're out in the deep *with* God. Often I know where I'm going, but don't know how to get there for an assortment of reasons. I might be scared of the unknown, or I might get my directions confused (I am directionally challenged even with a navigational device). We all have our own reasons for delaying what God has asked us to do. But I believe most of us desire His help to overcome all obstacles. Simple obedience gets me along the road more quickly. It's best for me not to overthink anything; like what might be or might not be along the course that enables me to accomplish my assignment.

The catapult was a great invention way back in about 399 B.C. It was used to launch any number of objects for both defense and attack. My imagination entertains the image of being catapulted to my destination. An immediate straight shot there. Once the slingshot liftoff happens, any excuses I may have will be left behind.

Most of us like to wade slowly out into deeper water and wait for our bodies to adjust to the temperature. Also, we want to make certain of sure footing, because we can't see the bottom of where we're walking; it's similar to faith. Then we get to our waist and have to go through the same routine again; another step of faith. Now we are up to our neck stretching it as much as possible with our chin as high in the air as we can get it. What a sight we must look like to God as we are making our journey through this life. With each challenge I face, I can see why God doesn't show me everything at once. I will gladly take my steps of faith, one at a time. He is the only one who truly sees our potential, and oh how much we need Him!

Only God knows what our future holds. This is a good plan if you seriously consider what you would choose to do if you knew everything beforehand. I believe my brain would absolutely short circuit if I were to see all that I would encounter and attempt during my lifetime. Our entire path is a school of learning that compels us onward. I like to call it my pilgrimage. It consists of failures and accomplishments every step of the way.

Without the failures, there can be no accomplishments nor would we know the difference. Press on.

> Now when he had left speaking, he said unto Simon, launch out into the deep, and let down your nets for a draught (Luke 5:4 BRG).

> Can you search out the deep things of God? Can you find out the limits of the Almighty? (Job 11:7).

> Then he took his staff in his hand; and he chose for himself five smooth stones from the brook, and put them in a shepherd's bag, in a pouch which he had, and his sling was in his hand. And he drew near to the Philistine (1 Samuel 17:40).

Chapter 26

Live While You Wait

Most waiting rooms are mundane and mind-numbing when waiting for our name to be called next at the dentist or doctor's office. I would much rather be doing something than nothing. So, I take a book to read, cards to write to sick friends, or birthday wishes to send, media information to catch up, and work on prioritizing my "to do" list again, which is always in need of adjusting. My best friend always has crocheting to do as she waits. I admire her beautiful work, but it's just not my cup of tea. The point is, we can all do something while we are waiting that is advantageous in one way or another.

We should live our lives like Jesus is coming tomorrow or even today. A good course of action is doing our best not to ignore our commitments. Leading a monotonous uneventful life just because we've read the end of the Bible is not fulfilling for anyone. Don't wait motionless, get things done, accomplish new endeavors, and contribute to humanity. Give attention to things in ourselves that need a closer look. Listening and being sensitive when God puts us in a quiet place prepares us for what to do next. When we are productive, it usually motivates others to be producers as well. Others see us living life to the fullest, and God's best can stir that desire in those around us as well.

We don't *do* things to get into heaven. We are doers, because we are about the Father's business. We are industrious Christians and responsible citizens, being productive as God directs us and works through us. Consider the advantages of good health: eating nourishing foods and participating in wholesome activities. Abusing ourselves is not advantageous to any goal. Just because we know Jesus is coming, we don't say, "Why bother? I will get a new body." That's silly.

Think of our lives like a menu or gym. We have free will to choose whatever we want. There's the fast food section, snack section, light section, four-plus course section, soup and salad section, drink section, and dessert section. Choose. How long on the treadmill, weights, jump rope, yoga, or kick boxing? Choose. How much of each is going to be the best balance? What do we need the most or least of? What do we need to start or stop?

Our intentions are good, but that does not always make them right. Choose well.

> Beloved, I pray that you may prosper in all things and be in health, just as your soul prospers (3 John 1:2).

> And He said to them, "Why did you seek Me? Did you not know that I must be about My Father's business?" (Luke 2:49).

> But those who wait on the LORD shall renew *their* strength; they shall mount up with wings like eagles, they shall run and not be weary, they shall walk and not faint (Isaiah 40:31).

Chapter 27

Oh Ye of Superpower

Our human abilities as defined in God's Word show us that we cannot do anything without Him. We as human beings dwell in our natural abilities. God, on the other hand, is the Supernatural, the Omnipotent. Superpower exists in the hands of superheroes only to entertain our imagination. As a mom, I remember that season all too well. I've seen some of those heroes, better known as children, dash through my house at lightning speed, grab a cookie, and jump off couches or chairs with capes flying high. Imagination and creative minds are of God, and they will learn soon enough the limits of their power.

The problem is we develop fleshly pride and consider it a chink in our armor to surrender our weakness to Him. It never ceases to amaze me how we reason that pride makes us think more of ourselves than we should. More accurately, it keeps us in spiritual trenches. Is it possible we are in denial? Oh, how it benefits mankind when we see beyond our pride, admit our shortcomings, and surrender our inabilities. God is our strength through our weakness. It's better to shine with God than try to outshine His supreme deity.

Some might think why bother turning to God for strength and endurance, if we are like a breath or a passing shadow? His Word asks us this question: He clothes the grass of the field so how much more does He care for us? We cannot see the words spoken out of our breath nor can we see words being carried on the wind. We cannot fully realize how words spoken to our brothers and sisters may change their lives. But if we are indeed speaking the breath of God's Word, we may find out when we arrive in heaven. *Arrive* is a meaningful word here. Many people believe they have arrived to their heavenly destination while here on earth. Of course, that's not possible in our earthly realm. The best we can do is yield to a life of excellence each day, advancing us to become more Christlike. My husband, who loves golf, has a saying about this. Seeking God is like golf; as long as you are advancing the ball, you are making progress.

There is a remnant of "life" existing within the worst of times for everyone. We must believe the good Word of God will penetrate the deafest of ears. From ear to ear, the wind will gather up the breath of His Word and carry it from season to season and generation to generation. Though we may be a fleeting shadow, how grateful we are that God does care for us in whatever season of life. Even a shadow is NEVER alone!

> LORD, what *is* man, that You take knowledge of him? *Or* the son of man, that You are mindful of him? Man is like a breath; his days *are* like a passing shadow (Psalm 144:3-4).

> Beat your plowshares into swords and your pruning hooks into spears; Let the weak say, 'I *am* strong.'" (Joel 3:10).

> Now if God so clothes the grass of the field, which today is, and tomorrow is thrown into the oven, will He not much more clothe you, O you of little faith? (Matthew 6:30).

Chapter 28

Peace: A Companion to Gratefulness

The peacefulness that surpasses all understanding is indeed good for our thirsty souls. Have you ever noticed that when we lose our peace, we tend to lose other things as well? Sometimes, I can spend so much time trying to understand a situation that my lack of peace leads to even more unrest. It's hard to "let go and let God," but that's exactly what will make the difference. Psalm 73:16 says, "When I thought how to understand this, it was too painful for me." One of my spiritual fathers once told me to not worry so much about what I don't know and pay attention to what I *do* know about Christ. This was a good lesson. Today, I practice that by imagining that I am putting my questions on a shelf, trusting that one day God will give me the understanding I need. Until then, I move on.

Time in prayer or engaging in conversation shows me when I am worried, because I can't seem to concentrate. I'm trying to solve something or make a decision with a feeling of frustration. Growing up, my mother would occasionally say, "Denise, you're so scatterbrained." I took offense to that. I guess it made sense though, because my voice would get louder and my arms would flail about as a glare of confusion swept over my face. I'd like to say I don't get that glazed look on my face anymore. But along with the fact that I can't seem to form complete sentences when I'm frustrated or excited seems to confirm the fact that I still do. My husband and son have a favorite comment: "Mom broke herself again."

I am thankful for the leading of the Holy Spirit, because I can tell when something is off. He causes me to ask myself this question: *Where is your gratefulness?* Yes, right in the middle of my disquieted spirit, I am supposed to be grateful. A great check point.

As Christians, I propose we can all be more appreciative for everything from the minutest to the most grandiose. What I recognize in prayer time is my grateful heart being wrapped with a bit of a self-deserving attitude. Gratefulness was taking a back seat while I attended my pity party. What we're being grateful for "in the moment" could still mean there is a dilemma of sorts we need to work through. The practice is this: strive to be grateful.

Praying for someone else's predicament sheds a light on our own suffering, which is many times not nearly as troublesome as we make it out to be. With respect to those who are in a desperate situation, it does not discount their need for prayer and solution. As we lift up others in prayer and cast our burdens on the One meant to carry them, our load becomes tolerable, and we begin to see more clearly. He will not give us more than we can bear when we do so.

> And the LORD God prepared a plant and made it come up over Jonah, that it might be shade for his head to deliver him from his misery. So Jonah was very grateful for the plant (Jonah 4:6).

> No temptation has overtaken you except what is common to mankind. And God is faithful; he will not let you be tempted beyond what you can bear. But when you are tempted, he will also provide a way out so that you can endure it (1 Corinthians 10:13 NIV).

Chapter 29

When Freshwater Meets Saltwater

The ocean's high tide flows in such a way over some areas of the world that it meets up with freshwater streams or rivers. We scarcely think about this occurrence and what it means. I'm certainly no scientist in regard to the ecological system, but I do enjoy thinking about the natural process of our environment on this planet as being related to my spiritual walk. God speaks to us individually. We need only to listen and be observant of our surroundings.

The church teaches about sin and righteousness, as well as what happens when the two intermingle. Every person and every ecosystem has been created profoundly. The common factor between the natural and spiritual is change. I know some of us don't like change because it's challenging. I say accept the challenge and expect good things to happen as the outcome of determination.

In the mixing of saltwater and freshwater, there is turbulence because when they meet, a change has to take place. Scientists call this an estuary, and it fuels some of the most productive ecosystems on earth, and also some of the most vulnerable.

Comparatively, with regard to sin and righteousness, people may look well and good on the outside, but this doesn't necessarily mean they are tranquil on the inside. What belies an outward calm is possible inward turmoil. Vigorous turbulence results when the velocity of both freshwater and saltwater reaches a certain threshold. When sin meets righteousness, the result is equivalent. Because I was made aware of this natural phenomenon, my eyes were opened to the consequences of sin and righteousness when merged. There is confusion and disorientation. When the transformation takes place, something new and profound emerges.

Hopefully, when transformation takes place, one's life is beautifully and wonderfully rearranged. This adaptation, with certainty, can be incredibly powerful. That is necessary because we are not merely meant to survive but thrive in the hope and future of God's promises. His plans are to birth incredible and fantastic futures through restructuring nature and his children.

Your life depends on the outcome of the tumultuous activity when sin meets righteousness.

> I call heaven and earth as witnesses today against you, *that* I have set before you life and death, blessing and cursing; therefore choose life, that both you and your descendants may live (Deuteronomy 30:19).

> Then God said, "Let the waters abound with an abundance of living creatures, and let birds fly above the earth across the face of the firmament of the heavens" (Genesis 1:20).

> I made you thrive like a plant in the field; and you grew, matured, and became very beautiful. *Your* breasts were formed, your hair grew, but you *were* naked and bare (Ezekiel 16:7).

Chapter 30

You're Exhausted! Or Have You Noticed?

This was a comment and question I was directing to my dear sweet husband, repeatedly. It seemed to fall on deaf ears, however, **not** to my surprise. Why do our husbands mention they're not feeling well, and then deny it? I suppose that's no different than when they ask us, "Honey, what's wrong?" and we reply, "Oh, nothing." We all prove inadequate in one way or the other in communication.

My husband, Richard, has the God-given ability to function in many areas at once and do them well. Me? Not so much. He knows how to say "no," but simply doesn't think it's necessary. A portion of our relationship is like this: He is the teacher, and I am recess. I'm the one who provides encouragement and reminds him to take breaks from his hours of study and work schedule. It's an amazing blend to our marriage.

Several years ago, my husband was engaged in Restoration class at our home two nights a week, a men's Accountability group, performing The Living Last Supper Drama, mentoring, church functions, our son's school activities, consisting of Karate, piano recitals, and Boy Scouts meetings. Oh yes, and a full-time job. At ninety-nine percent of these events, I was present. Richard, however, also had a great desire to support as many as he could, but we found the limit!

It sounds crazy, but thank God he came down with a cold so we could stop him! After he arrived home one evening, I noticed he was experiencing shortness of breath. This concerned me greatly. He was sitting rather peacefully in a big chair with a smile and said: "Jesus is with me, and He will take care of everything." I love the Lord, but seriously, I was struggling with that. I called the men of his Accountability group, our pastors, and our neighbor who was an Emergency Medical Technician. The examination revealed he was fatigued and his oxygen intake was low. You see, my husband was going to be fine, although he needed to realize there was a balance problem.

An entire team of pastors and friends had already invaded the hospital when we arrived. Knowing my husband's personality, they also came equipped with a strong "word" or two, for which we are never too old. One of the men from his Accountability group shared this:

> Richard, I have a vision of a platter set before you held by the hand of God. He is saying, "These are opportunities and all of them are serving Me in glorification of My name. I want you to take a look at the platter and choose some of them. What remains on the platter are assignments for someone else. It doesn't matter which ones you choose. The one's you select, delight in them, enjoy them, and upon their accomplishment, they will be productive or fruitful. The others remaining on the plate will be presented to someone else, allowing experience in their service to Me. Others have been praying and desiring to use their hands, feet, and voice to grow spiritually and tend to other's needs just like you do."

Great advice!
What does your plate look like?

> When Moses' hands grew tired, they took a stone and put it under him and he sat on it. Aaron and Hur held his hands up—one on one side, one on the other—so that his hands remained steady till sunset (Exodus 17:12 NIVUK).

> At that time I said to you, "You are too heavy a burden for me to carry alone. The lord your God has increased your numbers so that today you are as many as the stars in the sky" (Deuteronomy 1:9-10 NIV 1984).

> Have them serve as judges for the people at all times, but have them bring every difficult case to you; the simple cases they can decide themselves. That will make the load lighter because they will share it with you. If you do this and God so commands, you will be able to stand the strain, and all these people will go home satisfied (Exodus 18:22-23 NIV).

Chapter 31

Are You Willing to Give It Up?

A life without sacrifice is a life without investment. Let's face it; there will inevitably be choices that cost us something, somewhere, sometime. That which is difficult at any level becomes an investment. The good return comes later. An important question here is, "Are you willing to wait and persevere?" This means exercising patience. Ever notice that when you pray for more patience, God gives you tons of things that require it? Just think of the incentive you will reap in the underrated gift of patience by practicing it.

Our hope being in Christ will provide all that is essential while living a sacrificial life. This doesn't mean we live daily with trepidation or shrink back from life itself. Not at all! It means that we simply live with great consideration for others, as well as being kind to ourselves while maturing and enduring. Hope being acquainted with sacrifice is a powerful incentive to press on and through.

I've used an impactful yet simple idea for precious ones I mentor who are going through a crisis. Most important is the fact that by using this approach, I've witnessed effectiveness. Many times they come to me with tears, anger, resentment, confusion, or doubt, and it's understandable. Confusion and tribulation can be huge stumbling blocks.

I make a figurative offer by suggesting that in one hand they hold the "problem," and in the other hand, they hold "hope." Then I ask them to choose one. Gladly, hope is always chosen. It may not be with the greatest of enthusiasm, but hope **is** chosen. This is powerful because it unlocks a door otherwise seen as an impenetrable vault. The situation, no matter what it is, can no longer be under lock and key. Hope sheds its light, leading the way to the next step in getting through any difficulty. This is a helpful method worth repeating again and again until the situation is resolved.

Choice will follow sacrifice. Once we make the choice, we take the step. Walking hand in hand, these two actions make for a prolific and rewarding season as they promote one another. Sounds crazy, but they do. Usually, something is gained and something is lost or given up—something we never would have seen without making the sacrifice.

As we give up, postpone, or rearrange with a sacrificial attitude, we advance God's kingdom in our lives and those that surround us. This is sowing seed, radical seed, in the most heartwrenching times. God knows that we might not take the painful road because it's so hard; but remember, we are part of God's kingdom here on earth, and He is in control.

Hope is the refreshing and choice in all things.

> Then the king said to Araunah, "No, but I will surely buy *it* from you for a price; nor will I offer burnt offerings to the LORD my God with that which costs me nothing." So David bought the threshing floor and the oxen for fifty shekels of silver (2 Samuel 24:24).

> Therefore my heart is glad, and my glory rejoices; My flesh also will rest in hope (Psalm 16:9).

Chapter 32

Make an Exchange

Trade in that old stuff. Not only trade it in, but when you do, trade up! Make a good exchange. Get rid of those old wineskins and items that are ragged and shabby. Get something brand spankin' new, and never look back. I'm not talking about recycling here. I'm talking about thinking outside the box we're in—outside the clutter of confusion, the meddling mess, the heap that hinders, the litter that's bitter, and the muddle that's trouble. We don't want it anymore, because we want something better.

We are told when having a grisly day to do our best and *just* get through it, *just* hang in there, or *just* grin and bear it. Wouldn't it be a greater yield to be deliberate in considering a higher level of thinking? I choose to trust that God is able to bestow upon me more than *just* enough to get by. Think about how often we use the word *just*. Sure, it's fine to use in our grammar, but what I'm suggesting is to think about what it means in certain applications—like barely, hardly, scarcely, and slightly. Is that really what we want for ourselves, our family, our church, and our friends, or for that matter, for anyone?

When it comes to overcoming spiritual hurdles, the altar at church is one of the best ways. Take charge of those confounding and worn out ideas and deceptions. No one can tell you when you've had enough of them; you have to come to that epiphany on your own. Leave it at the altar and take God's promises with you. When you relinquish it, there's an experience of heaviness that leaves you. It's a sigh of relief. I think of it as emptying out my pockets. There's always junk in there. Many times I find the residue of stuff in my washer after doing laundry. Then I *have* to throw it out. Either way, make sure it leaves your possession and ready yourself for things in mint condition.

With that being said, at times it's difficult for me to rid myself of clutter. To clear my mind and prepare myself for some serious change, God challenges me to start with my clothes closet at home; the apparel I cling to for too long. When I'm clearing out a closet, it helps me clear my mind of unnecessary thoughts. It may work for you also. Clothes that are too small, too big, out of date, sale items that should have never been purchased in the first place or worn out (but comfortable) items. Comfortable is a key word here. If it's comfortable, why change it? Comfortable represents complacency, contentment, or sense of security—false security. One of my biggest reasons for wanting to hang on to things is the fear that I won't get anymore. Seriously, can God clothe me? God can't bless us with new, unless we rid ourselves of the old; and God does not run out of provision.

In my weakness, God has given me the strength to alleviate my burdens. Give them to Him! I often use the phrase "cast your cares, but not your responsibilities." Try to remember when you give something up, you have to do something in its place. That's the exchange—beauty for ashes. And that's more than *just* enough.

> To console those who mourn in Zion, to give them beauty for ashes, the oil of joy for mourning, the garment of praise for the spirit of heaviness; that they may be called trees of righteousness, the planting of the LORD, that He may be glorified (Isaiah 61:3).

Chapter 33

What Do Your Feet Look Like?

I did not inherit pretty feet; nope, not in our gene pool. My son has had the fate of inheriting the same insane feet. Have you ever met anyone who can pinch with their toes? That's us; we can actually pinch with our toes. You've heard of thumb wars, but you haven't seen anything until you have seen toe wars! We might not be the happiest clan about what our feet look like, but I am surely thankful we have them.

We are not meant to be still, not all the time anyway. Our feet carry us miles upon miles of mind-boggling journeys. Constantly, we travel, work, perform an array of physical activities, and help serve others in a multiplicity of needs. How many of us are grateful when someone else is serving us by meeting a need or simply blessing us? We don't care a bit what their feet look like, do we? So whatever your feet look like, try not to take them for granted.

When I was writing this, I had concerns for readers who may have a physical challenge. Maybe you have some sort of malady that doesn't allow you to walk easily or at all. Perhaps you are in a wheelchair or use a walker or cane. Maybe you are paralyzed or bedridden. Then, please allow me to say this with the utmost love and encouragement; however, you get around, *that* becomes your feet. If you are in a wheelchair, then your wheels become your feet. If you use a walker, then your walker becomes your feet. If you are bedridden, then your bed becomes your feet. What if you have no physical voice or sight? Your thoughts can be written, and they become your feet. Please get the visual of this. God has, is, and continues to use all His children who are willing. Are we a people who listen so we can hear the will of God?

Let this seep deeply into your heart. People challenged in some way can be used mightily. God touched my heart about this when praying for a sweet lady who had severe arthritis in her feet. In fact, the Lord woke me up a few days later with questions about all who live with physical challenges. Are they ineffectual because they have lost use of their feet or perhaps born with none? Is there nothing to anoint for greater purpose? Is there nothing to release through them? My response was, "Wow!!" All of us need to see beyond a physical challenge. God's Word is released through people in ways we cannot begin to imagine. He is creative, because he is the Creator, so "equip your feet" with courage and take the high road.

> Having shod your feet with the preparation of the gospel of peace (Ephesians 6:15).

> For as the body is one and has many members, but all the members of that one body, being many, are one body, so also *is* Christ (1 Corinthians 12:12).

> I have led you forty years in the wilderness. Your clothes have not worn out on you, and your sandals have not worn out on your feet (Deuteronomy 29:5).

> Yes, He loves the people; all His saints *are* in Your hand; they sit down at Your feet; *everyone* receives Your words (Deuteronomy 33:3).

> Do not let any part of your body become an instrument of evil to serve sin. Instead, give yourselves completely to God, for you were dead, but now you have new life. So use your whole body as an instrument to do what is right for the glory of God (Romans 6:13 NLT).

Chapter 34

Coloring Outside the Lines

D o you remember when you were growing up and trying so hard to color inside the lines of a coloring book? I look back on some of my son's artwork, and those first pages fit the description, "beauty is in the eye of the beholder." Okay, as a mom, of course it was bona fide artwork, and I even had the first giant one framed. A million coloring books later, he was overjoyed with his improvement, as he should have been. He practiced and got better with his own creations. To my joy, I was often greeted in the morning with a drawing of a person with legs and arms shooting right out of the head.

Alas, we all reach yet a new milestone. In discovering one of the constants of personal progress, I learned that people will, to varying degrees, attempt to keep within the lines or boundaries as they mature. Some we set for ourselves and some we understand are set by God. If He gives us an assignment, He has obviously opened up specific boundaries of operation. I call this our realm of authority. Think of a job or helping a friend when they specifically ask for help or volunteering at church or for your community. We know what our job description is, and it's important to stay within that scope. This in no way means we cannot implement a goal for promotion and does not mean perfection, it means strive toward our best. Any good leader walks in a communicative open forum for suggestions and comments.

When we operate outside our realm of authority, the atmosphere is disturbed, because it conflicts with another's responsibilities and their assignment. The operation can fall apart. There is a productive process in expanding your territory. We must first understand who we ultimately work for—and that is Christ. In serving and working, we are placed under some kind of authority. Everyone has a boss. There are many goal-setting ways you can choose to promote yourself or color outside of those pesky lines. A good reminder is that in order to excel, we must strive to work toward excellence. It is always advantageous to remember "not to burn your bridges" in making choices. I like to use the phrase, "sow where you want to go." You can achieve your goal by implementing good work ethics much easier than trying to cross a burning bridge while you're on it.

It is not man who ultimately promotes you; it is God your provider.

> And sow fields and plant vineyards, that they may yield a fruitful harvest (Psalm 107:37).

> As for the saints who *are* on the earth, "They are the excellent ones, in whom is all my delight" (Psalm 16:3).

> When they went, they went toward *any* of their four directions; they did not turn aside when they went, but followed in the direction the head was facing. They did not turn aside when they went (Ezekiel 10:11).

Chapter 35

Too Big for Your Britches

Knowledge is learning; wisdom is knowing when, where, how, or why we should implement what we've learned. The pursuit of knowledge keeps our minds sharp and gleans awareness for us. I believe it's vital to seek knowledge all the days or our lives with the same likeness as that of an accomplished student. My husband is a man of perpetual study. As of the writing of this book, he is 73 years of age, works a full-time job, received his bachelor's degree in criminal justice last year, and has been accepted into a master's program in the same field. He says that studying is his sanity from a long day's work.

Wisdom is imparted by God, and it accompanies knowledge and understanding. We can't pick up a book that teaches us how to acquire wisdom. Oh, sometimes I wish that were the case, but there are no shortcuts to gleaning judiciousness, not to my knowledge anyway.

During a time of personal study, I asked myself: *Am I being blinded by my own wisdom?* I dug a little deeper to collect insight. I don't believe we can ever have too much of anything that comes from God. I think what it means is that knowledge is running alongside the wisdom God gives us. Sometimes our knowledge wants to hold the same rank as wisdom. Could it be there is a power struggle between the two? The more knowledge we acquire, definitely the more acuity we need. So in Scripture, God reminds us that wisdom dwells with prudence. Again, let me say, that just because we know something doesn't make it wise to implement it.

The reason wisdom needs to dwell with prudence is because wisdom, I believe, desires to be held accountable. As much as we sometimes think we know it all, we really don't. What a rude awakening for some of us to find out that truth! This is an old fashioned statement, but my mom used to say to me: "Now, Denise, don't get too big for your own britches," which meant being too full of myself by thinking I knew everything. She was right, of course; I didn't know everything then, and I still don't know everything now.

I am reminded of King Solomon. There were many things he could have asked God for, yet he asked for wisdom and understanding. The Word shows me he had an unselfish heart and desired for himself those things that would profit him the most in leadership qualities for the people he served. I am drawn to people who have acquired wisdom, because they show me correct understanding of the knowledge I have. Seek not only knowledge for yourself, but also wisdom to share with others.

> I, wisdom, dwell with prudence, and find out knowledge *and* discretion. The fear of the Lord *is* to hate evil; pride and arrogance and the evil way and the perverse mouth I hate. Counsel *is* mine, and sound wisdom; I *am* understanding, I have strength (Proverbs 8:12-14).

> God gave Solomon wisdom and exceedingly great understanding, and largeness of heart like the sand on the seashore (1 Kings 4:29).

> Then God said to Solomon: "Because this was in your heart, and you have not asked riches or wealth or honor or the life of your enemies, nor have you asked long life— but have asked wisdom and knowledge for yourself, that you may judge My people over whom I have made you king" (2 Chronicles 1:11).

> Because He has inclined His ear to me, therefore I will call upon Him as long as I live (Psalm 116:2).

Chapter 36

Tension

Thank goodness there are clever people gifted to sew. Sadly, I'm not one of them. I have tried several times but with little success. In high school, we had a Home Economics class, which taught cooking and sewing. One year our assignment was to make a simple dress. My poor sisters and a few friends all received the same dress, accessorized with a potholder and oven mitts . . . all out of the same fabric! Needless to say that was my last attempt at sewing.

I could never quite figure out all the functions of my sewing machine, especially the "tension" knob! If the tension is set too loose, the stitches will not have a tight enough connection, and large gaps will result, as well as the fabric not holding together. If the tension knob is set too tight, the thread will get jumbled up and the sewing needle cannot seem to move freely. The right amount of tension, with a bit of stretching the fabric causes a stable connection between the two. The end result is that you have something that can be used and functions well.

There's another kind of tension that isn't related to a sewing machine, but it still involves holding something together. It's between family and friends, in the workplace, or at home, stemming from change, challenges, disagreements, or discipleship. Tension comes because we don't know how we will be affected by any given situation. Also, we are uncertain as to how something will be received by others. Will we approach the circumstances with too much pressure or not enough? What is the right amount of tension to hold it all together? It seems like we are sitting on pins and needles until we surmise the best solution.

When there is upheaval between our family members, it's extremely disquieting to say the least. Talk about bursting a bubble; it's like a magnificent Thanksgiving Day Parade when a big balloon character deflates right before your eyes during the procession. I just want to make it stop!

There are times when I've said (to God), "That's it, FINE!" I'll just add this one more thing to everything else that's happening. He spoke to my heart, saying: "It's one thing. Not one more thing. Stop adding them all together." It made sense. I cannot resolve all things at once. I certainly can't apply the correct mending solution to each thing when I'm overwhelmed. Whatever comes up daily, we should deal with and not heap one thing on top of another. I try not to let tension build with too many unresolved issues. It causes peace to run thin and functionality within the family reaches an all-time low. The Lord says He will give us no more than we can bear. Whatever we are facing today, God is our help and in the business of mending.

> Come, and let us return to the LORD; for He has torn, but He will heal us; He has stricken, but He will bind us up (Hosea 6:1).

> When He had gone a little farther from there, he saw James the son of Zebedee, and John his brother, who also *were* in the boat mending their nets (Mark 1:19).

Chapter 37

Trend Setters

Oh, how fashion changes—fashion in clothes, the way we conduct business, and how we relate to others. What's "in" one day can be "out" the very next morning. You find yourself behind the times and out of the loop, yet again. Does it matter to you? Are you a label person? Does what you wear define you? Don't get me wrong, dressing fashionably is fine, but whether you wear fashionable clothing or not is less a concern than how you treat others or how you think others identify with you.

God is interested in our fixation on all matters. Do we need a lot of money in order to have friends? How about that shiny new car? If we don't have it, will we not get the attention we're yearning to have? Any false desire leaves us empty and striving for more, because we are never satisfied. We are not to take for granted the good things that come our way nor be jealous of another's good fortune. Instead, know who we are in Christ, whether we have little or a lot. Then, we can be real, not pretentious.

I perceive, and hopefully comprehend, the reality of what I think I want compared to what I need. Simply taking a look at my bank account sets me straight. Living within my means is an important lifestyle. By doing this, we can actually plan, believe for more, and attain it. Let me tell you, I speak blessings over my checkbook! I believe for an increase to take place, especially when I need it. Also, I believe God wants me not to place limitations on what He can do in prospering my family.

God wants to bless us as any father would. As our son was growing up, we didn't wait until he was some kind of perfectionist before we blessed him. No one is going to be perfect . . . ever. We wanted to bless him as he was expanding his horizons, and we still feel that way today. Quite frankly, I am glad God feels that way about me. I need His encouragement and guidance, because I'm a mess at times. If I'm focused too much on what others have and what I do not, I will certainly miss what God intends for me.

Let's pull in the reins of comparison. We can't fit into someone else's mold and should not want to. Be the dynamic person God created you to be right where you are.

Let the proud be ashamed, for they treated me wrong-fully with falsehood; *but* I will meditate on Your precepts (Psalm 119:78).

For I consider that the sufferings of this present time are not worthy *to be compared* with the glory which shall be revealed in us (Romans 8:18).

I know how to be abased, and I know how to abound. Everywhere and in all things I have learned both to be full and to be hungry, both to abound and to suffer need (Philippians 4:12).

Chapter 38

There's Action Even If You're Still

My body says I'm still, yet my mind is traveling. This is kind of like daydreaming I suppose; sort of envisioning what I aspire to accomplish and the best way to get there. In this state of mind, we're looking at all possibilities and obstacles along the way and rerouting our plan as necessary before embarking on the train for an adventure. This method of travel gets me out of a rut. In order to boost myself out of a humdrum-downer day, it takes a little attitude check. I want to plan to do something other than attend the sister pity party to my humdrum day. And that's what will happen tomorrow, if I don't remove myself from the overhanging dark clouds of today.

Typically while at a standstill, we're busy cultivating our mind. We're gathering supplies and equipment to both plow and garner a harvest. God gave us a creative mind, so we might as well use it. When in one place, notice how you may have overlooked the obvious because of thinking there's nothing in need of your attention right in your own backyard so to speak. The desire to go to some faraway place seems to be more intriguing. But, you can't start "over there," you have to "get there" first. So, you must return and refer to the plan on the chalkboard of significant steps in your mind. Pray for clarity.

There's a great deal to connect within what I like to call my growing place of stillness. I am assembling my agenda considering how God is leading me. However He directs me, I am confident He will enable me. The truth is, if God authors something for you to do, He will enable you in body, mind, and spirit. He is already at that finish line of any task or dream with open arms waiting for you to get there. I'm so excited right now in writing this that I am cheering myself on for my next assignment!

Being in one place can be an extremely spiritual time. You're being sensitive to your surroundings and contemplating to a great extent. One of the most advantageous benefits you get from traveling in one place is allowing God to do the preparation. Have you ever known anyone who does so much they have to stop everything and mark it all incomplete? It's back to the drawing board for them. Being still before you embark will allow you to reassess as necessary.

Once you set out, you will be equipped and prepared for any traps of deception. The last thing you want is to be duped by hostiles. Be at peace and don't miss your train. While you're waiting to get your ticket stamped, simply relax and don't go off in some other direction, or I can guarantee that you *will* miss your train as my best friend and I literally did in Portland, Oregon. We stood in front of our beautiful train having our picture taken as it left the station without us. A joyful end is still in store for your accomplishment but there could be a delay. It was humorous though to see the photo of our smiling faces standing in front of the train we should have been on. Lots of plans don't always mean planning well.

> Be still, and know that I *am* God; I will be exalted among the nations, I will be exalted in the earth! (Psalm 46:10).

> The LORD said, "Look! They are one people with the same language for all of them, and this is only the beginning of what they will do. Nothing that they have a mind to do will be impossible for them!" (Genesis 11:6 ISV).

Chapter 39

Mirror, Mirror on the Wall

I wonder what it would be like to have a mirror that always said what I wanted to hear; that I'm the fairest in all the land, until one day it finally tells me the blatant truth. In a fantasy world, I might consider getting a brand new mirror, but in time I'm sure even the new mirror would tire of telling me how wonderful I am. We can't depend on fantasy to help us, so we depend on trusted ones in our lives to help us see clearly, biblically, and honestly.

The truth sometimes hurts, but even so, it's best to prepare ourselves to hear it. The testing element when hearing surprising or even shocking news about oneself is to ask the question: "Is there any truth to what I've been told?" A greater difficulty is accepting it and not being offended by a truthful fact. Arrogance, conceit, smugness, and self-importance want to rise up, and we may choose to turn away in a huff. Hopefully, we can embrace, consider, absorb the information, and move on to assimilate change for the better.

God has used others, specifically family and close friends, as a mirror to point out various methods and ideas deemed necessary for me to deliberately adjust a situation. I admit it takes soul searching but afterward I'm grateful, especially for the fact I have people surrounding me that dearly love me. After all, looking in a mirror and seeing an imaginary reflection of someone else instead of my own, telling me "something's gotta change" is humbling. Being able to communicate well in relationships is honoring to each other. This is a two-way street among relational people. Practicing a method like this makes it quicker and easier to accept good direction. Practice. Practice. Practice.

There is a tendency of wanting to lash out at the person who has, well let's just say, enlightened us about something we need to hear. The response goes something like this: "Well, what about when you . . . ? Or, how about what you did . . . ?" Blah, blah, blah. Don't let pride keep you from receiving godly direction. Be one step ahead; from time to time ask your closest friend to hold you accountable by giving you a summary of your day-to-day actions. In turn, and more than likely, that friend will ask you to do the same for him or her.

The Word says He will teach us in the way we should go. Oftentimes, He will appoint exactly the right person to share a word of wisdom in our ear. So let's listen with an inclined ear like one who is being taught; much like Timothy whom Paul sent to remind the church of the ways of Christ.

> For this reason I have sent to you Timothy, my son whom I love, who is faithful in the Lord. He will remind you of my way of life in Christ Jesus, which agrees with what I teach everywhere in every church (1 Corinthians 4:17 NIV).

> I applied my heart to what I observed and learned a lesson from what I saw (Proverbs 24:32 NIV).

> When pride comes, then comes shame; but with the humble *is* wisdom (Proverbs 11:2).

> Whatever you have learned or received or heard from me, or seen in me—put it into practice. And the God of peace will be with you (Philippians 4:9 NIV).

> Pride goes before destruction, and a haughty spirit before a fall (Proverbs 16:18).

Chapter 40

Emotions Run Amuck

That's what they do, and that's why we can't rely on emotions for assessment and resolution. At best, they are finicky, fickle, and frazzled, but on the other hand, oh how I enjoy the freedom of emotions that allow me to exude joy. I experience emotions that are both nerve-racking and blissful, because God has chosen to incorporate emotions into my being. It's up to me to discover how to experience my God-given emotions.

One of the ways to appreciate joy is to see it in others—their laughter, optimism, giddiness, or excitement. The spirit of joy is one of the numerous fruit of the Spirit, and it is a gift I can fully explore. Emotions can be vulnerable and timid, but they can break down spiritual walls between people. That's powerful. Emotions reveal what is underlying or hidden away when they are misrepresented. They are the brighter side of any shadowing conduit. Joy resides and is ready to be unearthed. The Lord tells us to have exceeding joy! Imagine what the world would be without it!

But how do we handle our emotions when in dire need of a solution? Those times when we can't think straight to even begin seeing a light at the end of the tunnel? A frantic state of mind is a mind without clarity, which is distracting to the issue at large. In those times, we have to get hold of emotions that are spinning out of control. Something is happening that is bigger than we are capable of handling. We shouldn't deny ourselves the moments of time to express our concern, whether it's crying, or screaming. My sister-in-law does this little dance where she jumps up and down screaming, "mee-mee-mee-mee." I know, because I've seen her do it, but then she's more than ready to deal with the task at hand. When my best friend is angry or tries to get her point across, she sometimes stomps her foot. I've seen her do this, and I can't help but laugh even though I know she's serious. The idea behind all this is to do what you need to do. Get a grip on a situation and be rational.

Now that we've moved on after this display of calamity, it's time to seek the qualified help we need. It's time to call on the One who is capable. The Lord can make a way when there seems to be no way. He hears our cry for help, even though we can only muster a whisper. His peace that surpasses all understanding will be our comfort and calm. We can jump for joy at that!

> Indeed these *are* the mere edges of His ways, and how small a whisper we hear of Him! But the thunder of His power who can understand? (Job 26:14).

> Be glad in the LORD and rejoice, you righteous; and shout for joy, all *you* upright in heart! (Psalm 32:11).

> He shall call upon Me, and I will answer him; I *will be* with him in trouble; I will deliver him and honor him (Psalm 91:15).

Chapter 41

Are You on Solid Ground?

Are you on solid ground, or is it shaking like an earthquake? Having grown up in California, I've experienced that eerie feeling. When the floor began shaking beneath my feet, it was odd and somewhat scary. As the quake intensified, a loss of balance made walking difficult. It was clearly abnormal for the ceiling lights to begin swaying in my home. It's a frightening thought to think I might find myself in danger of a falling structure and debris. You're never quite sure which way to run for safety.

Another thing about earthquakes is the inability to prepare for them. Unless you're a geologist, it's pretty much impossible to understand the natural phenomenon taking place below the earth. All I know is that what takes place underground by natural shifting causes an effect on the surface of our great planet. Science has achieved much in detecting an approximation of a quake's occurrence, but still there's not enough time to avoid the devastation. How grateful I was to experience only tremors resulting in little damage. The people living at the center of impact were not so fortunate.

Though we cannot prepare for an earthquake the way we would like, we can choose to prepare ourselves to be steadfast in our Christian life. There are things going on inside us all the time, non-stop. Even if we don't understand what they are, we can take measures to ensure we are thinking and expressing what we need in order to nourish our souls. When on rock-solid ground, everything seems to flow more smoothly. It's important to realize that what goes on in the inside eventually reaches the surface.

Should we come upon a person in need of help in an onslaught of certain trouble, it's much easier to assist or rescue them when the "tremor" is just beginning. However, a point comes when it is much more difficult. If we wait too long, we miss an opportunity to intercede on someone's behalf to assist them. Like the beginning cracks of an earthquake, the more rapidly we notice a danger sign, the better we can avoid pits and falling debris. With a rapid response we are able to steady ourselves and others with proper defense and protection when a shaking occurs.

Contrary to what scientists lack, God can equip us; He has no lack. The Bible does give us direction for remaining on the good path so our feet will not slip. People will take notice of us and follow our lead. We must make sure to lead in a way that goes to a safe place with a sure foundation in order to be healthy. Look around. Most everyone is grasping for something to hang onto even if it's a remnant of a stone to step upon.

Your outreached hand is an extension of Christ, so have strong ones.

> You enlarged my path under me; so my feet did not slip
> (2 Samuel 22:37).

> He lifted me out of the pit of despair, out of the mud and the mire. He set my feet on solid ground and steadied me as I walked along (Psalm 40:2 NLT).

Chapter 42

No Lurking Allowed

What's lurking behind the scenes in your life? If we don't find that something, it will assuredly find us. Anything that lurks is probably not something we want to encounter. Let's suit up in the full armor of God and expose it. We are an army, steadfast amid understanding the precepts of God. His idea is more than simply right or wrong; it's the precepts of why something is right or why something is wrong.

When my son first began speaking, our communication reached a new level. I always explained the "why" of right and wrong. I wanted him to understand, so I taught value. Obviously, there were times I had to pull the "mom" card and say, "Do this now" or "Stop doing that now." He developed understanding of such valuable lessons. Today, he's a young man of 23 years behind him, and once again, we have reached a new level of dialogue. He has a remarkable mind and penetrating communication skills. It isn't easy for him, but I'm grateful he chuckles when I need to use my "mom card" if we greatly disagree. My son can outscore me 95 percent of the time with strong debating skills, so I usually keep a card up my sleeve.

Awareness of a possible hidden agenda seeking to persuade us is opportunity to "nip it in the bud"; in other words, prevent it. When God reveals what is masked, we can then stand face to face in strength of what is targeting us. Being fitted with armor is for our protection, both on the offensive and the defensive.

I think Eve, while in the Garden of Eden, was the paradigm for hidden things. After she partook of the forbidden fruit, it initiated a particular standard set in motion. And we all know whom she learned it from. Unfortunately, people have been implementing this tactic of deception ever since, because some have an absurd view of right and wrong. Other reasons could be issues of character, personalities, upbringing, teaching, or unhealthy relationships. A big one is lack of understanding how to "fit in." The way we perceive others is askew. If we don't have understanding and awareness, we are unable to address what needs to be revealed. The positive is that people desiring changes are willing to come out of their hiding places.

Kind and sympathetic Christians are motivated to embrace and help regardless of any statistic. There is nothing quite as rewarding as watching someone open the door to their aching heart and receive assistance in support and wellness. The worst of things hiding in people can be exposed, giving all the opportunity to live in freedom.

> Then the LORD God said to the woman, "What is this you have done?" The woman said, "The serpent deceived me, and I ate" (Genesis 3:13 NIV).

> Therefore do not fear them. For there is nothing covered that will not be revealed, and hidden that will not be known (Matthew 10:26).

> Therefore take up the whole armor of God that you may be able to withstand in the evil day, and having done all, to stand. Stand therefore, having girded your waist with truth, having put on the breastplate of righteousness, and having shod your feet with the preparation of the gospel of peace; above all, taking the shield of faith with which you will be able to quench all the fiery darts of the wicked one. And take the helmet of salvation, and the sword of the Spirit, which is the word of God (Ephesians 6:13-17).

Chapter 43

There's an Elephant in the Room

How on earth did that elephant get in without anyone seeing it, and why is it that people take such great effort ignoring it? For goodness' sake, a blind person could see it! Seems like there's always someone making an attempt to disguise it, which is ultimately impossible. The more we try to hide it, the more ridiculous it looks, the more powerful it grows, and the more it defies authority.

Sometimes when I have something heavy on my mind, I will toss and turn before falling asleep. This must have been the case one night, because I dreamed a baby elephant had indeed gotten into our church; not sure when, but suddenly it was just there. I watched a lady trying to shove it under a table! That sounds about right, but it wasn't going to stay under there forever. Better to have removed it from the premises while it was small. Some dreams have a good message worth thinking about.

The so-called elephant in the room represents anything that is extremely larger than average, which is one of the reasons there isn't likely going to be people standing in line to take charge of the project. If someone is delegated the task, quite often they may opt to recommission the undertaking; also, known as "passing the buck." The best way to address the elephant is straightforward. The longer it's ignored, the larger it gets because somebody's feeding it. Removing it becomes nearly impossible without a tow truck and crane.

Speaking spiritually, how can we address what the elephant signifies? Let's say, the aforementioned elephant is in the church. When small, it can enter more easily without being noticed; like sin when it's small with an appearance of being insignificant. It takes up residence within the church body in various groups, leadership, classes, or volunteers. It becomes accepted within the congregation, though seeming a bit odd; we just can't seem to put our finger on why. Use your imagination here; if the elephant entered full size, its existence would be pretty obvious. Sin doesn't make an entrance like a full-grown elephant; it enters and goes without notice like a wee little mouse. As Christians, we need to address sin when it's small. We don't want to learn to manage it!

Strive to be a people determined with a mindset of equipping and empowering others to approach transgression which otherwise impedes them. Once we learn something, we can no longer claim ignorance. Keep in mind that ignorance is lack of knowledge compared to stupidity, which is foolishness. Gaining knowledge, we become accountable with responsibilities that require follow-up with action. Genuine love for others is the strength behind corroboration.

If an elephant is sitting next to you, guess what, it might be your "tusk" to tackle it head-on.

> Get up! Command the people to purify themselves in preparation for tomorrow. For this is what the LORD, the God of Israel, says: Hidden among you, O Israel, are things set apart for the LORD. You will never defeat your enemies until you remove these things from among you (Joshua 7:13 NLT).

Chapter 44

Light's Destiny

Light doesn't have a certain destiny per se but travels until it reaches an object. A great many lights we see in the starry night sky have been traveling farther and longer than I can understand. An astronomer I'm not, but I've read that light continues its journey long after a star has burned out, for hundreds, thousands, even millions of years. Can you imagine what light could illuminate in narrative form during its far-reaching path? It boggles my mind, and once again I realize God created a fantastic, endless, and heavenly sky without limits.

My family experienced the magnificence of alluring night skies during the time we lived in Brownsville, Oregon. Living on top of a mountain without distracting city lights, we were captivated by its brilliance. We had a beautiful deck that wrapped around our home with lots of room to place chairs, hammocks, and tents that we utilized to the fullest. One of our favorite things to do was arrange three big lounge chairs side by side, and then place three fluffy and warm sleeping bags on each of them; one for me, one for my husband, and one for our son. The dark backdrop of an infinite sky became illuminated and drew us in more than any manmade laser light show ever could. We watched in amazement as numerous falling stars shot across the never-ending expanse of sky. Also, it was fascinating to differentiate between airplane lights and satellites. The Milky Way captured us as it shimmered like glitter. Our eyes lingered toward the heavens for a long time before falling asleep under the illustrious night sky. Some nights my husband would set up a big telescope that expanded our vision and revealed planets. As I think back, it's amazing we were able to sleep at all contemplating the hand of God in all creation.

Natural light from starry skies doesn't have a destiny; it simply travels. But the One who sends forth spiritual light does indeed have perfect destiny. Intentionally, and through faith, the divine Word of God outlives any beam of light. Divine light upon reaching its destination permeates and expands with such an impact it would take your breath away if only our eyes could behold it. There is a way, however, to see the effects of divine light through means of God's people. Spiritual light brings with it an extraordinary presence that draws others to it.

Each of us is a symbol of hope similar to that of a lighthouse on the edge of an ocean cliff pointing the way in the midst of darkness and raging seas. Are you beckoning others and drawing them into safety? Are your words illuminated with the light that permeates the soul? God has set in place an exquisite world with an unfathomable expanse for all to enjoy. But I believe there is nothing more impressive than the beauty and value in each other. The light of Christ that shines through us is infinite.

> Then God made two great lights: the greater light to rule the day, and the lesser light to rule the night. *He made* the stars also. God set them in the firmament of the heavens to give light on the earth (Genesis 1:16-17).

> Let your light so shine before men, that they may see your good works and glorify your Father in heaven (Matthew 5:16).

> Give ear, O Shepherd of Israel, You who lead Joseph like a flock; You who dwell *between* the cherubim, shine forth! (Psalm 80:1).

Chapter 45

Cry of the Nation

The approximate 400 years separating the Old Testament from the New Testament are sometimes referred to as the silent years. They were anything but silent and would reshape the world forever upon the arrival of Christ our Lord and Savior. In closing the Old Testament, Malachi 4:5-6 says, in essence,

> The Lord is coming. These years were preparation for a new beginning. There is grounding in silence and waiting. Impatience is best left on the sidelines. Not doing so leads to deviation and disparity.

The governments of nations are continuously in need of the populous crying out in prayer. People are grasping for hope and truth for futures that belong to them. Division comes when the question arises: "To whom do you trust your life?" There is a remnant of individuals who know where their future lies.

The New Testament opens with political overtones much like we are experiencing today. When you listen to the news and see the crumbling of society, where do you turn? We see man glorifying man, yet destroying mankind. Who can fix that? Who can take the disarray and confusion and make sense of it? How can finite man attempt to do the infinite that only God can do? There is one answer and that is to put your trust in God. Men may be able to remove the phrase "In God We Trust" from anything they choose, but trust in God cannot be removed from our hearts.

Our nation was founded on the Word of God. Nowadays, venues continue surfacing with an agenda attempting to remove truth. The pockets of people remaining faithful collect their strength and powerfully advance to other believers and stick like glue. If you can imagine the planet Earth like a dot-to-dot sphere, you can see God's amazing connection throughout the globe. They gather like stones to the embrace of God and the Word says in Matthew 3:9: "And do not think you can say to yourselves, 'We have

Abraham as our father.' I tell you that out of these stones God can raise up children for Abraham" (NIV).

If you think your voice doesn't matter, remember there's someone out there who is looking to unite his or her voice with yours. Strengthen yourself with others having the same innate desire to grasp hold of truth and not live by the world's crazy standards that are ever changing. Wrap your mind around the One upon whom you can depend as you position yourself at a point of preparation to embrace others of like minds.

> "For I know the plans I have for you," declares the Lord; "plans to prosper you and not to harm you; plans to give you hope and a future" (Jeremiah 29:11 NIV).

> By myself I have sworn, my mouth has uttered in all integrity a word that will not be revoked: before me every knee will bow; by me every tongue will swear (Isaiah 45:23 NIV).

> For out of Jerusalem shall go a remnant, and out of Mount Zion a band of survivors. The zeal of the LORD will do this (2 Kings 19:31 ESV).

Chapter 46

Love the Unlovely

Beauty lies in the eye of the beholder. This paraphrases what Plato said in 429 B.C. and is commonly verbalized today. I often use that phrase when viewing pieces of art with a friend whose likes and mine are poles apart. Thank goodness we have other similarities! Appreciating a distinction in the art world is relatively harmless. People have different likes and dislikes. That's one of the great ways we complement each other. We are uniquely designed, and because of that we are a reflection of our surroundings. The fact that we express our differences is validation that we are using the creative mind God gave us.

When it comes to relating to people, our opinions should take on a more insightful point of view. We can't set a piece of artwork free to be what it really is, because it is what it is and you either like it or you don't. When it comes to people, it's a whole different story. People are unbound to enjoy a surplus of God's bounty, and people are not inanimate objects. I'm sure you've heard the phrase "You can't judge a book by its cover." That being the case, we must see more than appearance and look deeper than a first impression. Have you ever discovered how much you liked a person after you got to know them a little more? Contrarily, you may have been drawn to someone at first then come to realize you had more differences than you first thought. Like I said, dealing with people is different from dealing with pieces of art. To put it simply, we should not base our relationships the same with people as we would in the world of art. Mankind is beautifully and wonderfully made and set upon this earth with dominion over all. There is a harmonious blend between preferences. Likes and dislikes merge together in a mix that works. How dull life would be if we all preferred to be the same as everyone else.

There is another, Jesus Christ, greater than any, who said: "Love one another," not "things." He did not tell us to love by description or category, nor did He tell us to compare ourselves to others. In fact, He tells us not to compare. He simply said love one another and that it is the greatest commandment.

Let's be in agreement, having a greater desire to see in people beauty instead of ashes; healing instead of sickness; strength instead of weakness; heart instead of cruelty; acceptance instead of rejection; wholeness instead of brokenness; encouragement instead of discouragement; and acceptance instead of rejection. Unlike a painting, a person can indeed be set free from things that suppress them. There's considerably more beneath the canvas of a person. If we all had artistic abilities, it would be eye opening to see everyone's self-portrait. Ask God for that revelation in others.

> And now abide faith, hope, love, these three; but the greatest of these is love (1 Corinthians 13:13).

> Then God said, "Let Us make man in Our image, according to Our likeness; let them have dominion over the fish of the sea, over the birds of the air, and over the cattle, over all the earth and over every creeping thing that creeps on the earth" (Genesis 1:26).

> We do not dare to classify or compare ourselves with some who commend themselves. When they measure themselves by themselves and compare themselves with themselves, they are not wise (2 Corinthians 10:12 NIV).

Chapter 47

Feeling Lost?

You may not have noticed the erroneous turns landing you in mysterious territory. It would be amazing if at birth if we came with a map detailing everywhere we are supposed to go, when we were to go, and why and how to get there. But more than that, details of what we would encounter in transit would be helpful. That idea always sounds good when we're in the midst of being lost, but let's think further about it.

I think blazing a trail is part of mankind's experience. Sure, if we could foresee the future, we wouldn't have to wonder about anything; but we would miss so much of each excursion. My best friend and I took a cruise of the Hawaiian Islands. We certainly wouldn't have considered staying on board ship when pulling into an island port. That's crazy! Even though we read the brochure beforehand about what the island had to offer, staying aboard ship would never do; we wanted to visit the new land—hands on. Brochures stirred up eagerness to see everything we could with excitement and anticipation. That's what life is about. Can you imagine being given a map of the world when you were born and that was it; that's all you were ever going to see—a map itself? Well, our spiritual walk can be similar because God wants you to embrace life to the fullest, not simply think about it.

Unknown territory for me was when my son was born, and I was wide-eyed about everything. The selection of "How To" and "Self-Help" books I perused were helpful, but they fell short in areas pertaining to strategies of what was to come. I discovered my number one "go to," and most foundationally reliable without fault, is the Bible.

As a mother, I wanted to encourage my son to live well and embrace life. We all question at one time or another, our abilities, choices, and decisions that come with our God-given free will. The thrill of the journey is always going to be risky. If you notice your road is bumpy, rugged, and harsh, it means you're off the main road a bit. When you find yourself too far from where you should be, there are several things you can do. The first is, recognize what your situation or state of mind is. Second, toss pride aside, and third, make the decision to start over if necessary. With God, we can always begin again.

Enjoy what is meant to bring you joy. With God's help, don't be fearful of the unknown; be ready for it!

> And when he comes home, he calls together his friends and his neighbors, saying to them, "Rejoice with me, for I have found my sheep which was lost!" (Luke 15:6 NASB).

> A time to scatter stones and a time to gather them, a time to embrace and a time to refrain from embracing (Ecclesiastes 3:5 NIVUK).

> For His anger *is but for* a moment, His favor *is for* life; weeping may endure for a night, but joy *comes* in the morning (Psalm 30:5).

Chapter 48

Shackled in Chains

Freedom is better. Getting older, I notice in greater specifics the details of words in conversation. I hear all too often the remark, "It seems like I have chains tightening around me so much I can't move." This comment is non-specific to age, and it saddens me to know precious people who feel this way. With shackles and chains, you have no vision of how to get beyond a certain point. Your strength is also zapped from you. Think of how many people in the world today are visionless because they are hopeless. Some people are trained to live this way. If they are fortunate enough to gain freedom, they're fearful of stepping outside the area of their confinement and ultimately shrink back in timidity. They have been wrongly conditioned, and though they could escape, they may never do so.

Prisoners are either incarcerated by physical boundaries or bound within their own spirits. Either way, the God of the universe can sever chains that bind you. It doesn't matter what shackles you. You can choose to break those chains with a saturation of God's promises that are directly spoken to you within His divine Word. Tell others how free you are with Christ by your side. How you feel should not define you or your capabilities.

From generation to generation, we pass things forward; some are helpful and some not so much. Many people have shared this remark with me: "Well, that's the way I was raised, and if it was good enough for me, it's good enough for you." Sound familiar? This says there is no willingness to change and improve. With sincere hearts, we should desire for our children to accomplish more than we have, and it begins with a pure heart.

I reflect upon my mother's life and how different her upbringing must have been. Maybe some of you can relate. She didn't talk about "stuff," but instead she had a motto of, "out of sight, out of mind;" and she would simply move on. Her main priority was taking care of us making sure we had what we needed first. One summer I decided to give my mother's bedroom a makeover. As I involved myself in the project, I came across a little book, *How to Raise Your Children*. It was tucked away like some big secret. No one was there to help her deal with her own problems much less help her raise us except that frayed little book. Sadly, she was bound. I remember well all of her efforts with great love.

Instead of remaining in a prison, release yourself, and then release your children to be everything imprinted upon them by the hand of God. Don't expect your mistakes to be theirs; they are free and certainly capable of making brand new ones. I don't believe it's our children's responsibility to make restitution for our mistakes. Better to encourage them as they press on by being their own best advocate.

> For which I am suffering even to the point of being chained like a criminal. But God's word is not chained. . . . Those who cleanse themselves from the latter will be instruments for special purposes, made holy, useful to the Master and prepared to do any good work (2 Timothy 2:9, 21 NIV).

> Stand fast therefore in the liberty by which Christ has made us free, and do not be entangled again with a yoke of bondage (Galatians 5:1).

> Very truly I tell you, whoever believes in me will do the works I have been doing, and they will do even greater things than these, because I am going to the Father (John 14:12 NIV).

Chapter 49

A Wall for This and a Wall for That

Is it time to build a wall or tear down a wall? Look around you; they're everywhere. Depending on what's at stake, a wall can be to your benefit or ruin. Imagine for a moment life without walls. I imagine this would be very confusing to say the least. Think of walls as assigning territory. They are a fortress and give protection. There are also walls erected to prevent, rather than allow what's actually meant to enter.

When the Israelites left Egypt, the Lord built a wall of water to protect them as they crossed the Red Sea, escaping Pharaoh. The wall of Jerusalem lay in ruins, so King Solomon raised a labor force to rebuild. These exemplify times to build.

On the other hand, people of Israel marched around Jericho for seven days, and the walls came crashing down (Joshua 6). This chapter signifies the difference between God's way by faith and the way of man by his own strength.

At times, we are motivated to tear down a wall and start all over. Or, we may opt to add on to what we have without considering whether we need to or not. More of something doesn't always fix a problem. The tendency here is that it confounds instead. Maybe there's a need to get rid of some things. I like the phrase "let go and let God."

From time to time, I erect a wall in my own life without always realizing I've done so. On the other hand, I may let down a wall because of poor judgment. At various times, I may establish a spiritual wall to keep things in and another moment create a wall to keep things out. Periods of being overwhelmed can lead to confusion. Confusion can then lead to languish. This halts effectiveness and causes radical and haphazard structure.

If we're faced with what seems to be insoluble odds, a good idea is to look at our structure—both where we live in our home and our spirit man. You'd be surprised what a good spring cleaning will do. House cleaning is an excellent way to begin in both of these areas. Be willing to ask God for revelation of what you are promoting in your spirit, as well as what you are promoting in the home. What do you need to remove? Our goal is to sweep dirt out, not under the rug. The key is not to leave the clean area empty, creating a void. Let's replace the meaningless with fruit of the Holy Spirit that exudes a sweet aroma.

> To everything *there is* a season, a time for every purpose under heaven: . . . A time to kill, and a time to heal; a time to break down, and a time to build up (Ecclesiastes 3:1, 3).

> *God is* wise in heart and mighty in strength. Who has hardened *himself* against Him and prospered? (Job 9:4).

> Then it says, "I will return to the house I left." When it arrives, it finds the house unoccupied, swept clean and put in order. Then it goes and takes with it seven other spirits more wicked than itself, and they go in and live there. And the final condition of that person is worse than the first. That is how it will be with this wicked generation (Matthew 12:44-45 NIV).

> Now Jericho was securely shut up because of the children of Israel; none went out, and none came in. And the LORD said to Joshua: "See! I have given Jericho into your hand, its king, *and* the mighty men of valor. You shall march around the city, all you men of war; you shall go all around the city once. This you shall do six days. And seven priests shall bear seven trumpets of rams' horns before the ark. But the seventh day you shall march around the city seven times, and the priests shall blow the trumpets. It shall come to pass, when they make a long *blast* with the ram's horn, *and* when you hear the sound of the trumpet that all the people shall shout with a great shout; then the wall of the city will fall down flat. And the people shall go up every man straight before him" (Joshua 6:1-5).

Chapter 50

Copy Cats

D o you remember playing the game of copying whatever one of your friends said or did? I don't know about you, but when one of my friends did that to me it made me almost blow a fuse. Silly, but I had a hard time ignoring them. Being stubborn children that wouldn't quit, our voices escalated which was usually followed by a ruckus. Seriously! Over what? Eventually, an adult pulled the plug and that was that. Sure, it started out fun, but when an adult walked into the room, someone was going to get it. It's funny how what began as a game evolved to no good end. Fortunately, as forgiving children, we were resilient to just about anything and would soon be best friends again. Oh, if that fine trait only remained throughout our lifetime.

As schooling advanced, the next tendency to copy one another became a bit more risky, copying each other's papers during class—still to no good end. Cheating doesn't make us smart it postpones our intellect. You might have been like me, the one who always got caught giving away the answers, again, to no good end. It's not that I was so smart; I just wanted to help my friends if I could. If you weren't my friend, I wouldn't give you the answer. As I review this behavior today, I wasn't helping my friends at all; I was enabling their bad study habits. The ones I wouldn't help were the ones that excelled and probably still do. When we were children, we spoke, understood, and thought like children, but there comes a time to put childish things away.

Maturing moves us onward down the road to carve out for ourselves the inevitable likelihood of becoming and acting like an adult. We still play the game; however, it's less noticeable or less up-front you might say. The culprit today is, to a great deal, a comparison to someone else. We want what they have, and we will do anything to get it. We don't care what they did to get it we simply want it. Often, we desire to walk in their achievements to such a degree it becomes our sole purpose. We lose sight of our own triumphs that could be in store for us. Further, we unfortunately forget what our ideals were.

Sharing and receiving essential information is advantageous as we pursue our ambitions, but we must realize what our own methods, contributions, and goals are. They may not be what someone else's goals are, nor should they be. Make sure you're not the one cheating yourself! God's design for you is to be creative in your own right. There is nothing created that hasn't already been created. He has put everything we need within arm's reach for us to be resourceful and to make good use of it.

> Let no one cheat you of your reward, taking delight in *false* humility and worship of angels, intruding into those things which he has not seen, vainly puffed up by his flesh mind (Colossians 2:18).

> When I was a child, I spoke as a child, I understood as a child, I thought as a child; but when I became a man, I put away childish things (I Corinthians 13:11).

> He found him in a desert land and in the wasteland, a howling wilderness; He encircled him, He instructed him, He kept him as the apple of His eye (Deuteronomy 32:10).

Chapter 51

Ask the Right Question

Seek, believe, and knock, and you will find doors opened to you on a daily basis, regarding all things. As a rule, pray that what you are asking is indeed with veracity and goodwill. This is healthy for spiritual prosperity. The Word will never lie to you, lead you astray, or abandon you. The Word will forever teach, strengthen, enlighten, and be your shelter. One question I ask is: 'How can God be glorified?" If I'm able to truthfully check my motive, I will assuredly get the answer that aligns with my responsibility. Even if it's not the one I want, it's more than likely the one I need. Taking "me" out of the equation makes for a direct pathway to God's best. People, no matter what condition they're in, can glorify God; they simply may not recognize it in themselves.

Asking God a question is different from getting someone's opinion. One is being directed to the author of all things, and the other is like asking "a jack of all trades." If you've never heard that phrase before, it's someone who knows a little bit about a lot of things, but doesn't usually excel in any particular area. It's not a bad thing, and it's great to know a little bit about many things; it's just not always the best source to seek answers that need specific depth. When addressing others in search of an answer, we may keep asking around until we hear something from someone who agrees with us. This doesn't mean it's correct; it means it sounds good and is something we can live with. Something we can live with? I don't believe God's plan is for us to simply settle for anything. A few good questions here are: What are we attempting to do? and What do we really believe the outcome should be? The correct answer is what we ought to require.

I know of an amazing horse ranch in Oregon called Crystal Peaks Youth Ranch. You can check this ranch out at www.crystalpeaksyouthranch.org. Based on the love of Christ they pursue rescuing Equine, mentoring children, and offering hope. It's a beautiful pairing of spiritually and physically broken people with abandoned and abused horses. Amazingly, horses are kindhearted and responsive, often choosing the person who needs them most. This ranch was only a dream at one point in time. The original condition of the property required having tremendous imagination that would inspire their faith to see the transformation before being completed. With diligence the property would be raring to go and used for healing the broken. Even when bewilderment reared its ugly head at such a momentous task, in the end, the land was miraculously replaced with a dream which came true. Hard work and exhausting persistence was accompanied by the right question being asked. It was not, "Lord, what have I gotten myself into? Get me out of this situation." Rather, "Lord, what do you want me to get out of this situation?" See the difference? Jesus teaches us to ask the correct question.

> Ask, and it will be given to you; seek, and you will find; knock, and it will be opened to you (Matthew 7:7).

> God is not a man, that He should lie, nor a son of man, that He should repent. Has He said, and will He not do? Or has He spoken, and will He not make it good? (Numbers 23:19).

> Now as *Jesus* passed by, He saw a man who was blind from birth. And His disciples asked Him, saying, "Rabbi, who sinned, this man or his parents, that he was born blind?" Jesus answered, "Neither this man nor his parents sinned, but that the works of God should be revealed in him" (John 9:1-3).

Chapter 52

In Retrospect

Our future is a compilation of our history. If ever you doubt where you are spiritually, stop for a moment and take a look at how far you've come. Maturing can be problematic, and some of those I've mentored wonder why this is so. I think it's how we mature that's key. How can we tell if we are getting something right if we don't get a few things wrong? Mistakes are not purposed well when used as an excuse to proceed haphazardly, but we should not be embarrassed or ridiculed by blunders and bloopers either. We must learn from inaccuracies and not waste them. If we begin learning from the bumps and bruises at a very young age, the more we will mature in a well-adjusted manner.

When my son was a toddler, he experienced growing pains like most youngsters do; both emotionally and physically. I prayed: "Lord, please keep the bumps and bruises small as he learns to adapt." I didn't want him never to experience pain because that's unrealistic. Things were going to happen that would be painful. What I believed for was that he would get something out of the mistakes he made and learn the better way to accomplish his goals. As he got older, I prayed the same. Even now, as a young man, I pray the same. Small mistakes lead to something. They lead to not making huge ones! To a great degree, his level of maturity is developed by what he learns from past mistakes.

The obstacles now are quite a bit different from when he was a toddler; for example, when he wasn't tall enough to bump his head on the corner of the kitchen table as he ventured under it. Then one day, he suddenly had an encounter with the corner. It was quite a surprise to him! But I turned it into a learning experience of growth. Some things he could no longer do, but at the same time, new things were coming his way as he grew taller. He learned to estimate what he was walking under and duck if necessary. A toddler's age is only the beginning of learning how to foresee incoming obstacles; best to remember that tactic as an adult.

What's over and done is not trivial by any means, but essential in compelling us, if not thrusting us into the future. Compel yourself to go through mistakes as one of your greatest learning experiences. Let's face it; we gain wisdom in addition. Don't dwell on what you haven't achieved or accomplished. Finish each season well, because that's how you will begin the next. God will not waste any of our past or pain. Once victory prevails, He reveals to us His reasons for allowing such experiences to have stormed our lives. That's when we begin to smile and recognize His presence all along. That's retrospect at its finest.

Choices set in motion cause unlimited destinies. Many circumstances are out of our control, yet many are within our knowledge of better thinking. When we endure and live to tell the tale, it's the very thing that hopefully prevents others from going through the same anguish and misery. I believe we are our brother's keeper, walking alongside to help set their sights in the right direction. Solving their problems is not our responsibility, but we encourage them toward the One who can. Just remember to "duck" occasionally as you proceed with caution.

> Do not rejoice when your enemy falls, and do not let your heart be glad when he stumbles (Proverbs 24:17).

> For whatever things were written before were written for our learning, that we through the patience and comfort of the Scriptures might have hope (Romans 15:4).

> I, therefore, the prisoner of the Lord, beseech you to walk worthy of the calling with which you were called with all lowliness and gentleness, with longsuffering, bearing with one another in love, endeavoring to keep the unity of the Spirit in the bond of peace (Ephesians 4:1-3).

Chapter 53

A Mother's Love

Many times the Lord has awakened me to pray. I admit there are times I lack obedience, but then conviction convinces me that I must arouse myself out of my sleepy state and pray. When He awakens me in the middle of my nightly slumber and beckons me to get up and pray; I do so with anticipation because there is a sense of urgency. When I don't, the day begins with a tinge of regret, and that's no way to greet the dawning sun. Upon awakening and spending time in meditation, I look forward to what my day brings. Prayer never fails.

I don't know if I had grandparents that prayed for me or not. I was only able to spend a few short years when I was a child with my mother's parents and my Dad's father. Today, I know many grandparents who pray continually for their children and grandchildren. My plan is to be a grandmother who prays; I can tell you that. I believe in it so strongly that I have already begun praying for my grandchildren just like I prayed for my son before he was even born. It's never too early to begin praying for someone or about anything. There's something liberating about prayer. It's a releasing and receiving at the same time that I cannot explain. But my faith knows.

I reflect on incredible women in my life that have educated me and still hold me accountable. What would the world be like without the love of mothers and their spiritual guidance? That is something I cannot fathom. God's Word says about love; it's the greatest commandment. There is nothing that outshines its resolve; even if unto a bitter end. Love brings peace, imparts wisdom, shrouds us in strength, teaches with patience, encourages the downtrodden, enables the fainthearted, births natural life, awakens a dead spirit, gives itself away with no expectations—and humbly love receives love. Love is always fashionable and love finds the one that seems to be lost in a field of many. Love indeed says many things, but it never ever says "you may not enter here." Love seeks its own level like water and finds a way. There is always a remnant of love in the hardest of people, and a mother can find it. She knows it's there. Mothers stir and fan the flame of love igniting it to spread like wildfire.

First Corinthians speaks measure upon measure of greater understanding pertaining to what love is and the power it holds. A mother's love should never be underestimated. Love is a conqueror and builds strength, because love is also a weapon to fight for what is true. I have seen mothers restore love like the missing piece of a puzzle. God guides her heart to exude healing in brokenness and loneliness. A mother's love points out prideful nonsense and teaches how to weave knowledge into wisdom. Love is paramount to the goodness we release out of ourselves that awakens the same in others. Our lives are on a pilgrimage searching. When love is the catalyst, we more easily and quickly find truth. To all mothers, I humbly say, "Thank you."

> Your mother *was* like a vine in your bloodline, planted by the waters, fruitful and full of branches because of many waters (Ezekiel 19:10).

> Watch and pray, lest you enter into temptation. The spirit indeed is willing, but the flesh *is* weak (Mark 14:38).

Chapter 54

Selective Blindness

It's related to selective hearing; humorously, the kind my husband has. It must run in families because I think my dad suffered as well. I've gotten wise to selective blindness at home because the guys "claim" they can't find anything in the fridge or in the cupboards. Do they not live in the same house? It's like I rearrange things daily to keep them confused. Even so I still can't stand it when I hear someone say "Where's the "whatever?" I'm compelled to run to the rescue.

With respect and sensitivity, to those precious ones born without hearing or sight it is without a doubt, challenging; even with today's technology. However, if you have noticed like I have those beloved ones do not want our pity. Trust me, they are gifted in amazing ways and we should opportune ourselves to learn a great deal from their challenges. Remember God sees the entire person. Though none of us have all the answers as to why certain things happen we do know plenty about the goodness of God and how he loves and cares for us.

Spiritually speaking, selective hearing and blindness is part of our course. Ever wonder why God wants to commune with us; because it's how He reveals the plans for our lives if only one step at a time. We can't handle much more than that if we want to progress well. I believe He shields our eyes and closes our ears at certain times to protect us. It's well to pray like this; God show me what you want me to see when you want me to see it and open my ears in the same way. Part of our not seeing and hearing is because we are in preparation. God doesn't respond when we think its best, He responds when He knows what's best.

We must give it a try to understand ourselves as best we can. That can be more difficult than you think. The "rubber meets the road" when hard stuff comes our way. Encountering bumps in the road, our prideful mind tricks us to thinking we know best and a short cut looks real good. We possibly make a decision to alter from what we know is right as we turn a blind eye and deaf ear to what we know we must face. Do we really believe something goes away if we ignore it? Oh, sometimes I want that to be true but when I come to my senses I realize it's better to be done with a stumbling block once and for all and never camp there again.

Stubbornness is self-inflicted leading us astray and we might just get what we think we want. Let's not be the person who doesn't obey the voice of teachers that instruct! Resigning yourself to recognize the Voice of God is always in your best interest.

> In that day the deaf shall hear the words of the book, and the eyes of the blind shall see out of obscurity and out of darkness (Isaiah 29:18).
>
> My son, pay attention to my wisdom, turn your ear to my words of insight, that you may maintain discretion and your lips may preserve knowledge (Proverbs 5:1-2 NIV).
>
> So I gave them over to their own stubborn heart, to walk in their own counsels (Psalm 81:12).

Chapter 55

Rise and Shine

During a complicated and difficult time for my husband and me, a dear friend called us with this word of encouragement. He said: "Jesus waits to see your precious faces each morning as you awaken to begin your day." What a blessing to have friends walk alongside you no matter what's going on. Sunny days or cloudy skies, you know they're with you to encourage you, listen to you, and point you in the right direction when you can't see with clarity. It isn't that we are placing our trust in them above God; it's that He has given place in our lives for companionship as we blaze our trails through an all-terrain life. Just like we can't see to drive well and safely in foggy weather, neither can we see well nor make good decisions when our minds aren't clear.

Almost daily, smiling, I think of what our friend said to us. As believers, we are able to see the splendid wonders of creation every day with enthusiasm. At times, we must exercise our free will to choose the view for the better when we don't want to get up and engage the day ahead of us. No matter what our personality or what kind of morning person we are, God is consistent and wants to spend the day with us. Some people talk first thing, like me. My husband says it's like I never stopped. Others do not want to be spoken to at all until they've had a cup of coffee, showered, or exercised. Regardless, it's a new day! Whatever God allowed in my yesterday was preparation for something today. If yesterday was troublesome, don't let that rob you of today's events. There's freedom in Christ. You are not at the same place as yesterday and most assuredly don't have a ball and chain around your ankle from which God cannot free you.

How I look at it is like this: The past was a teacher that improved my future. I have learned to not be ashamed or afraid of it. I recall a time driving in the country, communing with God, and I simply gave all my past to Him—the good, the bad, and the ugly of it. I said: *"God, I believe You are going to use my past to help others. When You ask me to look back, You will enable me to draw from it which can now be seen with clarity. No longer will I be hindered in any way, but strengthened to help others in their Christian quest.*" I have been walking this out for quite some time, and I have seen the truth in it. When God spoke to me that day it resonated with my soul and I kept it.

God will speak to you at the weirdest times and when you least expect it. I believe that's when He knows He can get our attention. If you take a moment, consider the times you have been doing something and you thought you heard a small voice—a thought that helped you solve a problem, or suddenly realize something you had not thought of before. You probably weren't even thinking about it; it just came to you. Realize who's helping you. Start your day with the Most High, and you will notice how much He loves spending time with you. You have 24 hours, so get up and make it count!

> Then He said, "Go out, and stand on the mountain before the LORD." And behold, the LORD passed by, and a great and strong wind tore into the mountains and broke the rocks in pieces before the LORD, *but* the LORD *was* not in the wind; and after the wind an earthquake, *but* the LORD *was* not in the earthquake; and after the earthquake a fire, *but* the LORD *was* not in the fire; and after the fire a still small voice (1 Kings 19:11-12).

> *It is* better to trust in the LORD than to put confidence in man (Psalm 118:8).

> Therefore do not worry about tomorrow, for tomorrow will worry about its own things. Sufficient for the day *is* its own trouble (Matthew 6:34).

Chapter 56

Return to Innocence

Ever want to go back to a time before you knew so much? Or at least be selective of the knowledge you sought but still gain some experience? I don't think that's possible but there is a way to restore ourselves to a place of innocent-likeness because there is freshness and genuineness to innocence. It's like a blank slate. If only we were like a chalk-board and could erase away what went awry. That would be the easy way I suppose. God can do complete work instantaneously by performing miracles in us but often times He does not because He sees us in the bigger picture. He sees what affect we can have by fine tuning our mistakes a step at a time. When we resolve to this method, the accomplishments affect a multitude of "watchers." Those people who are waiting on the side lines to see how we direct our steps and words. I know; we forget about that fact some times. We are an example and there's no way around it.

Life is similar to a maze; upon entering we must find a way through. If we've experienced something that seems familiar we may attempt to retrace previous steps. Either way, hopefully we'll make progress. If we give up, realization sets in that back-tracking is going to land us at the exact same place we started yet still be empty-handed. Our pursuits would seem to be for nothing. With that being the case we haven't really gone anywhere, gained or shared anything or helped anyone. Most importantly we haven't paved the way for others. We must find the peaceful landmark that makes restitution with regard to our experiences. The reason being, experience has the potential of being excruciating as well as being identified with satisfying results. Let's face it; no one has to recover from correct decisions so we want that which we do to be of benefit.

We live in a fast-paced world today. That's both a blessing and a detriment to us. I think rather than re-do something making it better we often leave it in dilapidated condition moving on to something else. This makes the chances pretty great that we will repeat the same mistakes over and over again. We cannot do things the same way hoping for different results.

Fortunately we serve a restoring heavenly Father who sees us with uttermost undeniable affection and concern. There isn't one encounter without his awareness, be it virtuous or flawed. His vision for us is like that of a perfect and unique designers' blue print which is fashioned for us specifically; a workable plan that at some point is modeled for others. Our tendency, being of the human persuasion, is to "collect" everything and keep it "just in case we need it." Our lives would eventually be like pulling a moving van behind us where ever we went! He is the one and only one who can show us what we need and He alone can lighten our load by ridding us of items irrelevant to our goal. God is in the business of helping us get something right no matter how many times we get it wrong. Let the Lord give you back your innocence but with experience that is wisdom enriched.

> and said, "Assuredly, I say to you, unless you are converted and become as little children, you will by no means enter the kingdom of heaven (Matthew 18:3).

> Let us examine our ways and test them, and let us return to the LORD (Lamentations 3:40 NIV).

> Jesus replied, "Your mistake is that you don't know the Scriptures, and you don't know the power of God" (Mark 12:24 NLT).

Chapter 57

Between Hearts

The distance between hearts, relationally speaking, transcends any land or water mass. Isn't that a marvelous wonder, especially when we have friends and family living afar and we miss them deeply? When our family moved, we did so in a big way—from the west coast of Oregon to the eastern mountains in Tennessee, leaving behind many loved ones. I have asked the Lord to place authenticity between kinship lasting a lifetime. Throughout the years, I recognize He has done that in gratifying ways— one that has led us down new and unique roads. Our prayers for each other flow naturally in awareness of the other, remembering shared laughter in joyous times, as well as tears in gloomy times. We are "weathered friends" as one of my dearest friends often points out. The endurance of tough storms in both our families is not without reminders of the need to focus on the pristine views of glorious skies.

How do we avoid cracks that develop into huge fissures when miles apart? It helps to be creative in ways to close the gaps before they become huge fissures; otherwise, it's impossible to connect like we used to. We can no longer have them over for dinner, or attend church together, walk in the park, have a game night, chat for hours, or simply go to the movies together. Ask yourself this question; is the relationship worth the effort? I want to go with a yes answer here. Maybe it's not going to be easy, but you won't be sorry. We can still handwrite letters or cards and send by "Pony Express" mail—one of my all-time favorite ways of keeping in touch. Today's technology allows us to Skype, Face Time, and video each other to keep in touch. There isn't anything more valuable on earth than relationship. Yet, it is possible for them to slip away without realizing it.

I believe God understands when we miss our families and friends. He even understands when we move away from Him. If we are not as close as perhaps we once were, He desires us to remember. When we find ourselves distanced from God, we must bear in mind it isn't God who moves away. He teaches us how to nurture relationships despite the fact there is distance. Think what it must have been like to actually walk with Jesus physically right by his side! He spoke and taught avidly about remembering, so that when He left, ascending to heaven, people would be able to carry on in a new way with the comfort of the Holy Spirit's help. Christ is lovingly resident in our hearts. What a fine place to reside as a friend.

My heart was broken to leave so many people I loved. I made up my mind that I would do special personal things to let them know how I missed them and their wonderful influence on my life. Do you need to write a note or make a call today? Or, perhaps you want to be reconnected to the One who resides in your heart and misses you.

> Clearly, God's promise to give the whole earth to Abraham and his descendants was based not on his obedience to God's law, but on a right relationship with God that comes by faith (Romans 4:13 NLT).

> Two *are* better than one, because they have a good reward for their labor. For if they fall, one will lift up his companion. But woe to him *who is* alone when he falls, for *he has* no one to help him up (Ecclesiastes 4:9-10).

> A friend loves at all times. And a brother is born for adversity (Proverbs 17:17).

Chapter 58

Who Tracked in That Mud?

Living in the country, we were surrounded by dirt, rocks, pine needles, and mud—like clay after a rain. Winter or summer made no difference; whatever was outside wanted to come in. I didn't know you could track in a snowman though! I guess that happened because sometimes ours had additional ingredients if there wasn't ample snow to make a totally white one. No matter, we proudly embellished our snowman with twigs, leaves, and dirt.

For recreation, our son often had friends over. When it was time to come inside, it was "shoes off" first thing. Otherwise, that conglomerate of nature I mentioned would faithfully travel in attached to shoes as a reminder of what a fun day everyone was having. One particular day after a bunch of us came in, there was nature in all its glory on the floor. I checked everyone's feet, and come to find out it was me who tracked in mud! I failed to take off my shoes first thing. Fingers pointed to the shadow-like substance surrounding the soles of my shoes. Oh yes, I was the culprit and the precious ones standing there, whom I had accused, did not mind in the least pointing it out to me. The most outspoken one said to me, "Ms. Sherriff, you taught us to always take off our shoes and put 'em right there." No other response from me would do except an apology, followed up with a big hug, a thank you for listening, and food, of course.

When someone points out our mistakes and we are not offended, that is a good sign of maturity. When it's little ones calling us out, it's more humbling than offensive. I'm not talking about an adult being corrected in a smart-alecky way, but simply in a respectful manner. Simply wearing a WWJD (What Would Jesus Do?) bracelet doesn't cut it. What does count is action. Our audience is waiting for not just any response but the humble, honest, and correct one. It's inspiring to notice the good we teach is actually being learned. I used to ask in exhaustion: "Why is everything a teaching moment?" This is the profound answer I came up with: "It just is."

To get me jump-started in a right direction of responding to various situations, I need to recall what the Bible tells me, and one of things is to humble myself and turn from my evil ways. Now, I really don't see myself as evil. But remembering Scripture gets me to a place of relinquishing any smugness I may be harboring, allowing me to assimilate an appropriate attitude much quicker. Taking too long, we sometimes start justifying wrong behavior instead. It's likely we may notice this in later years with our children. If we justify **our** incorrect behavior, we won't like it much when we see them responding to us in the same way. I have learned that I can say anything, but it's my actions that teach.

A humble person is more teachable and approachable. The quicker we bring ourselves down a notch the better off we are. As we do this right thing in the sight of the Lord, He can make our mistakes like they didn't even happen. Be a person that learns from mistakes, no matter the individual whom God sends to teach us.

> [If] My people who are called by My name humble themselves, pray and seek My face, and turn from their evil ways, then I will hear from heaven, forgive their sin, and heal their land (2 Chronicles 7:14 HCSB).

> Whoever loves instruction loves knowledge, But he who hates correction is stupid (Proverbs 12:1).

> Talk no more so very proudly; Let no arrogance come from your mouth, for the LORD *is* the God of knowledge; and by Him actions are weighed (1 Samuel 2:3).

Chapter 59

The Battle Is His; the Choices Are Ours

That's the simple formula for a victorious outcome. Best choices are not always the obvious, and many times we are bombarded by distractions which come at us like darts from every direction as we try to keep pace on the front lines. We look from side to side accessing who is running the race with us—mutually equipped soldiers with the desire for victory as well. They have the same vision, and it's our team comprised of friends, family, and whoever else we sense our allies to be. They've been tried and tested and the true spiritual warriors remain with us. We may get a few scars along the way, but they will be our reminders of being champions. We live to tell the stories from generation to generation. Who doesn't love stories like that?

Think of those around us; let's call them our running mates. Some haven't fared well in the trials of fire, but we should be optimistic on their behalf. Endurance through trials can be very heated until things come to the surface. I compare this procedure to what silver goes through in the purifying process of heating it over and over so that all impurities come to the top and can be removed. It's important to not discount people who have only briefly touched our lives. Everything happens for some reason, and there is a season for all things. It may not have been their time for one reason or another to connect longer, and releasing them to God continues the good work in them and us. They will be tested again and persevere. I plan to spend the rest of my life in a spiritual fire that continues to purify me. I want to gain strength and be even more able to stand my ground no matter who my adversaries are. One victory leads to another and again becomes a generational mindset for God's kingdom.

There are people who have been praying and searching for a divine connection they can reach out to and join up with. I am hopeful I can be there for them and be ready at a moment's notice to embrace them and bring them into the fold. There are also those people who seem to run up to us, with a baton in hand, passing it on without even slowing down. These saints seem to have come out of the clear blue sky and know exactly where they're going. We are never alone in our pursuits to lead triumphant lives.

If we could see all that is coming our way, we would see both the need for preparation and the venue to celebrate. God isn't going to allow us to see as He does. We were not made to perceive such things. Our course of action is to live daily by laying the groundwork of preparation with a mindset to celebrate victories.

God's plan for us is constantly in motion, and He is involved in all aspects of all matters. Never is God taken by surprise. When God reveals something to us, it doesn't always mean it was just created. It means God merely revealed it to us at that particular time. I believe God has great joy as He watches over us and showers us with things that are new like a shimmering sky at the dawn of a new day.

> Then all this assembly shall know that the LORD does not save with sword and spear; for the battle is the LORD's, and He will give you into our hands (1 Samuel 17:47).

> But he said: "*It is* not the noise of the shout of victory, nor the noise of the cry of defeat, *But* the sound of singing I hear" (Exodus 32:18).

Chapter 60

Good Morning, Lord, It's Me

*L*ord, I awaken my heart to You. Cleanse it and fill it with prayer for my appointed ones. Be specific and increase my desire to be continually sifted like wheat, removing the chaff. Empower me to rise up and hold fast the two-edged sword that defends the Word of God spoken through Your chosen vessel.

That's a powerful alarm! How can I even think of pushing the snooze button?

When I greet my Maker each morning, I am spiritually nourished. If I have not rested well, it makes no difference, because the process of learning has taught me that it's the best way to begin. I don't want to choose to do so because it's on my "to do" list; I want to because I have a relationship with the Almighty that draws me near to Him. He is available to me, and I can ask Him to make the amount of sleep I had to be sufficient. I can choose to have a mindset that is proper to change the atmosphere—tired or not.

The Enemy desires to deface the property of God—His people; to make them faceless and lacking in purpose; to make them expressionless and dead—even while they're alive. Reading the Book of John tells us otherwise. Let's speak powerful awakening words out of our mouth as we encounter our regimen of the day.

Have you ever had your spouse, or anyone for that matter, say good morning in a cheerful way and your reply was something like a sarcastic, "What's so good about it?" How did the day go then? My experience when I have made an inconsiderate remark like that because I wasn't feeling up to par, set the day on a downhill course. It's like a door slamming shut and having a domino effect on anything that follows. I imagine God notices when I slam the door, when the only thing He wanted to say was, "Good morning; I care about your day."

We are to move into position though not without opposition. Let's pray:

Lord, make me along with others a strong core of people to oppose the upheaval that has for a season been able to push back and drive away authoritative godly presence. Standing on the Word of God, I say that season is over. A mighty wind is preparing to rush through. Warring angels will replace man's gates! I am curious, God. How big are they, Lord, those warring angels? I can't imagine the area, width and height they cover! They are angels of battle, liberty, and victory. God, I know You would not have given this expansion without an army, seen and unseen, the natural and the supernatural. I am ready for my day. Amen.

The thief does not come except to steal, and to kill, and to destroy. I have come that they may have life, and that they may have *it* more abundantly (John 10:10).

Arise, shine; for your light has come! And the glory of the LORD is risen upon you (Isaiah 60:1).

Awake, my glory! Awake, lute and harp! I will awaken the dawn (Psalm 57:8).

Chapter 61

Do I Belong?

Yes, you do belong, whether you realize it or not. This reminds me of a wanderer— someone who has been unwanted and dejected perhaps their entire life. What a terrible bottomless pit for any of God's children. Perhaps you've experienced rejection in your workplace or maybe never had close ties with family or friends. Being chosen for participation is right up there with some of the best things that can happen to us. I believe the hardest and toughest of people have an innate sense to belong. In reality, this may be one of the reasons gangs or cliques are formed—those who feel they want to be somebody no matter what it takes.

You may think it silly, but I remember my grammar school physical education class. When it came time to choose teams for an activity, many jumped up and down yelling, "Choose me, choose me!" Unlike me, they were the ones who scored points with ease most of the time. Plain and simple, it was always awkward for me, waiting to be chosen. I was usually last unless one of my friends happened to be team captain, but regardless, I cheered with the best of them anyway. Experiences like these are meant to strengthen, not destroy if one knows who they are in Christ.

I have several dear friends who have gone through the arduous process of adopting children. I witnessed the heartache as they would get their hopes up while the process seemed to be moving forward; yet for one reason or another, it would abruptly halt. In the end, perseverance would win. They had an abundance of love to give away, and throughout the world, there are countless children who want and need to be the recipient of a family bond. Every adopted child has grasped the importance of being chosen. The precious children who were adopted have lives that are enriched and walk fully in their God-given gifts. There are adversities to overcome in most families, but there are none too big to conquer. I can't be sure, but the children my friends adopted may have had a different outcome without this particular family choosing to love and raise them as their own. It's been a true miracle to witness, and it has encouraged others who have the same dream to adopt.

Well, people of God, guess who our official team captain is? Jesus Christ, and He indeed has chosen you. Christ was bruised, beaten, rejected, and crucified on the cross because He wanted to adopt you. He was persecuted, and He walked lonely roads in preparation for the ultimate sacrifice to demonstrate how much He wanted you and how much you belong to Him. The Bible tells us that belonging to Christ is our indication of being true children of God. Therefore, we are His heirs, and all of God's promises belong to us also.

> They are Israelites, and to them belong the adoption, the glory, the covenants, the giving of the law, the worship and the promises (Romans 9:4 ESV).

> But of Him you are in Christ Jesus, who became for us wisdom from God—and righteousness and sanctification and redemption (1 Corinthians 1:30).

> But you *are* a chosen generation, a royal priesthood, a holy nation, His own special people, that you may proclaim the praises of Him who called you out of darkness into His marvelous light (1 Peter 2:9).

Chapter 62

Freshen Up

When you feel downtrodden, there's nothing like a breath of fresh air to revive you. Stop for a moment, take a step back, sort through the heaviness of the day, the discrepancies between people, unanswered questions, and above all, find a quiet place to pray. Whew! You've done the right thing, and you will see more clearly when you get back to your assigned workload of the day. Your ability to be a vessel has returned. Once again, you can be used to bring refreshing to others since you yourself are refreshed.

That's what Paul did after he was appointed an apostle, preacher, teacher, and God's instrument. Paul, more than likely, had to deal with the same attitudes we do today. He was grateful to his friend Onesiphorus, because of how he ministered to him and often revitalized him. He was a true friend who saw beyond Paul's chains. We also are God's instrument, and Paul tells us we are to hold fast to the pattern of sound words he teaches with faith and love for Christ.

It's amazing to me what rejuvenates me the most when I can't quite seem to get traction on what I need to be about. I have discovered that what motivates me is helping someone else. I make someone else more important than myself. This is healing therapy. It isn't very long before my problems are minimized. Sometimes, I feel foolish at how pathetic I might have seemed and how dismal I thought my outlook was.

Have you ever met anyone who didn't seem to be "about" anything? We met an amazing artist in Hawaii on one of our opportunities to visit there. She had a family member that, according to her, had a difficult time managing day-to-day responsibilities. As we discussed the situation, she commented, "She isn't about anything." I asked what she meant. Her reply was, "Nothing ever stirs her heart to do anything for her own good or anyone else's, and days are continually empty." We both shared a poignant moment mulling over the thought that nothingness could be a shroud over anyone.

The daily grind of life doesn't have to be "run of the mill" and without joy for any of us. All we need to do is adjust the focus on how we see our surroundings. Changing the view seems to always be a pick-me-up. When

I'm attending my own pity party, all it takes is a single thought of someone else. If you don't care for your state of mind at any given time, God has pre-arranged a method for you to change it.

> But You, O LORD, *are* a shield for me, my glory and the One who lifts up my head (Psalm 3:3).

> Let nothing *be done* through selfish ambition or conceit, but in lowliness of mind let each esteem others better than himself (Philippians 2:3).

> When I remember these *things*, I pour out my soul within me. For I used to go with the multitude; I went with them to the house of God, with the voice of joy and praise, with a multitude that kept a pilgrim feast (Psalm 42:4).

Chapter 63

Scared? Don't Be!

Obedience to God will outweigh any fear we have. The Word says that fear is not from God, yet it will come. Each and every time fear is in our face or whispers in our ear, we can choose to reject it. Our faith then becomes more deeply seated and fierce. Who doesn't want faith like that? We have free will to choose what we are going to do and believe. When we overcome fear, we find the gift of wisdom awaiting us, as well as a sigh of relief. There is a cost to obedience, however, and it is better that we think of it as an investment. Choosing the correct way of thinking is not always easy. But, we must do so in order to not languish in fear that can immobilize us. What we say to our children—obey me because it's for your own good—is not unlike what our heavenly Father tells us.

When children are little, most experience fears of some sort. Remember, God gave us imagination; and because of that, a child can typically add the bizarre to anything that is even a little questionable in their minds. Some fears can be worrisome, and some we know will simply be outgrown as they mature. For example, when our son was a little guy, about five or so, he became fearful that his bellybutton was going to come undone! I'm not exaggerating! He had determined that his bellybutton was the knot that held him together. This went on for several months. He was in swim class, and each time he had to jump off the diving board, he would check his bellybutton to make sure it still had a knot in it. If he was jumping on the trampoline, he had to check periodically to see if he could still jump as high as he wanted without body parts flinging everywhere. It was funny at first, but then it became a worry for him. Though we questioned him, we never discovered why he thought this. But one day he decided the "knot" was as good as any knot a Boy Scout could tie. It was all over as quickly as it had begun. That's just one of my stories, and I'm sure you have yours as well.

Think of everything you've ever been afraid of for a minute. I hope you realize how far you've come from early childhood fears. As an adult, I have learned to look at fear as a challenge, and it takes courage. Fear also comes in the form of temptation. Maybe you have never looked at it that way, but if you do, it may help you guard against that fear. Most of us have heard the phrase, "don't give in to temptation." Well, you can shout it to the top of your lungs: "I will not give in to fear by way of temptation!"

Fear that crops up in us today must be approached with a knowing, belief, and trust that God's promises are forever true and can never be broken. "He is not a man that He should lie" (Numbers 23:19). Whatever has made you afraid, try to think back before it happened when there was no fear in you.

> For I, the Lord your God, will hold your right hand, saying to you, fear not, I will help you (Isaiah 41:13).

> Fear not, for I *am* with you; be not dismayed, for I *am* your God. I will strengthen you, Yes, I will help you, I will uphold you with My righteous right hand' (Isaiah 41:10).

> Blessed *is* the man who endures temptation; for when he has been approved, he will receive the crown of life which the Lord has promised to those who love Him (James 1:12).

> Say to those with fearful hearts, "Be strong, do not fear; your God will come, he will come with vengeance; with divine retribution he will come to save you" (Isaiah 35:4 NIV).

Chapter 64

Who Did Jesus Run With?

A s Christians, we stumble, fall, and roll along, making our way night and day right beside others of the human race. Among the commotion, we tend to get off track yet are drawn back in where we can make sense out of our toil and laborious struggles. We walk amidst unbelievers, scoffers, profanity, thieves, murderers, liars and many a corrupt people, their world collapsing in upon them. Who do they turn to? Are they not aware of God's compassion for them? The human factor here is, we like to use the word "they" before we use the word "we," or "me," when fault finding.

My husband visits a district prison on Sunday mornings before church to share a message with men about Christ. I have heard him ask the question: "Who did Jesus run with?" If we remember the unkempt, misguided person we might have labeled a deviant, it would be good for us to close our eyes, remember their face, and think, *Yes, Jesus did run with wayward ones.* Remember that even the disciples deserted Jesus. Mark wrote: "Then all the disciples left him and fled" (Mark 14:50 NET). This gets to the point very quickly for my husband to share about who Christ is. Then he often gives his testimony, and they know he can relate to them. Here is mention of a few that Jesus ran with.

- Matthew, considered to be an unjust tax collector (Matthew 21:31 NIV).
- John, son of thunder, a man with an explosive temper and an intolerant heart (Mark 1:20; Mark 3:17 NIV).
- Judas, who would betray Christ to fulfill prophecy (Matthew 26:14, 16).
- Thaddeus, an intense and violent nationalist with the dream of world power and domination (Matthew 10:3; John 14:22 NIV).
- Peter, a Galilean, a man of sedition, quick tempered, quarrelsome and impulsive. Strong's Greek: 749. ἀρχιερεύς (*archiereus*)
- Philip, who wanted to help others, but couldn't see how it could be done (Acts 21:8 NLT; John 6:5-7 NIV).

- Simon the Zealot, the Zealots were known for their hatred toward the Romans (Luke 6:15 NIV).
- Thomas, known as Doubting Thomas (John 20:25 NIV).
    —Adapted from *BibleInfo.com.*

Who I am today is not who I was. I don't think you are either. Reading about the disciples who walked with Christ teaches me a great deal about who Jesus was, is, and always will be. At various times, the disciples were uncertain. But Christ, well, He knew them all completely. Imagine that, a Carpenter from Nazareth.

Are we not the church being drawn to people hanging by a thread? Do we pray about bringing in the lost, but then size them up as being unacceptable? Pray the prayer of Jabez with meaning. The broken are ripe for hearing and seeing the true loving nature of God. Instead of watching a decaying and withering away of brothers and sisters, enlist your servitude as hands and feet of a loving God.

> Then He said to them, "Follow Me, and I will make you fishers of men" (Matthew 4:19).

Chapter 65

The Road That Leads Home

A nd the door is always open! What good would it do for a loved one to come home and find they could not come in, especially on purpose? It happens, unfortunately. When my loved ones have been gone for a while, I have one thing in mind—flinging the front door wide open to greet them.

If we turn a loved one away, there's a good chance they will have to return to the road and find a door that is open for them . . . any idea where that might be? This is an opportunity to dig deep and find out what the real barrier is in our own home. If it's not a physical door, it's the door of the heart. When a barrier is erected, it's not what we really want. This happens because we don't know how to disarm it. My question is this: How can I call someone "loved one" if I'm not willing to show them love?

Our children, perhaps away at college, come home with new ideas that very often are not what Christian parents have instilled in them. Their personal journey is unfolding at their fingertips with each new riveting step they take. As parents, trust in the seeds you've planted. Remember paper maps? When I opened up one of those, I could not figure out how to get where I was heading to save my life, even knowing where I wanted to go! Technology has changed all that. Wouldn't it be worry-free if we could install a Global Positioning System into our children so there was one best path for them, and we knew exactly where they were at any given moment? Be careful how you answer that question.

As loving parents, we must understand that our faith is not necessarily that of our adult children. Our children must find their spiritual path for themselves. Until they are of age, we diligently implement the best guidance we can muster; it has nothing to do with a navigational device. It has to do with loving and instructing with composure. Loving is never wrong, nor is it intrusive. Of course, there are other contributing factors, but impatience will mess you up every time. I've made many mistakes as the domestic engineer of my home, along with my family of coworkers, but do you know what? Love and forgiveness have walked hand-in-hand and will always prevail, because I know full well who my Counselor is.

Turn away from ideals that lead to regrets. When family members welcome each other it's therapeutic to the soul.

> Train up a child in the way he should go, and when he is old he will not depart from it (Proverbs 22:6).

> The son said to him, "Father, I have sinned against heaven and against you. I am no longer worthy to be called your son." But the father said to his servants, "Quick! Bring the best robe and put it on him. Put a ring on his finger and sandals on his feet. Bring the fattened calf and kill it. Let's have a feast and celebrate. For this son of mine was dead and is alive again; he was lost and is found." So they began to celebrate (Luke 15:21-24 NIV).

> And these words which I command you today shall be in your heart. You shall teach them diligently to your children, and shall talk of them when you sit in your house, when you walk by the way, when you lie down, and when you rise up (Deuteronomy 6:6-7).

Chapter 66

Within the Gentleness of a Mother, You'll Find a Bear

W hen it comes to our children, you better beware. There isn't anything a mother thinks she can't do when it comes to protecting them. More than likely you've heard stories of sudden strength coming to people in emergency situations verging on the catastrophic. That's a mom for you. There's no time to think about whether you can do it or not. You become all action and no words. I've seen petite women jump right in to confront someone who may tower over them when it comes to the protection of their children. Fear takes a back seat to strength, as it should. Doing so, we make ourselves available for God to accomplish incredible things through us. Think of it as a terrific motivator. Have you ever done something and didn't know how you did it? As a mother, that's the bear inside I'm talking about.

The Book of Judges tells us about Samson, a man of superior strength. His strength was a gift from God, and what he was able to accomplish was not by his own power. When I'm able to do something far greater than what my own natural abilities are, I'm experiencing what God is doing through me. It often happens in a split second. I think it's quick, so we won't have time to overthink our limited natural abilities. Take a second to think about something extreme you've done. If you scrutinize the situation too long, you may fail to follow through with a necessary action.

The most physically trained strong men, have a limit to what they can do. The ones who tap into what the Lord wants to do through them allow greater feats to occur. Whether you're a 98-pound weakling or a 400-pound powerlifter, the true source of who you are and where your strength comes from is dependent on knowing who Christ is in you. As a Christian, I want to call on God for whatever I need in any given situation. I want to walk in a Spirit-controlled temperament as much as I can; like I believe Jesus did.

I have been frightened to the point I couldn't speak, much less scream. I thank God something rose up on the inside of me that felt like I could topple a building. Physical strength enabled me to help our son during a visit to New York. With many sights to see, we utilized their main source of transportation—the subway. People were pushing and shoving as we boarded. We were separated, and I was pushed in. Then it happened. The subway door closed on my son as he was entering behind me. He was only six. I didn't even consider the fact that he would be fine with the group we were traveling with who didn't make it on that same subway car. There was not a person standing when I reached him and pushed open the door. He was terrified and my head was swimming in the thought of him being left behind. That scare only happened once during our visit to New York.

> Be strong and of good courage, do not fear nor be afraid of them; for the LORD your God, He is the One who goes with you. He will not leave you nor forsake you (Deuteronomy 31:6).

> I can do all this through him who gives me strength (Philippians 4:13 NIV).

> But his bow remained in strength, and the arms of his hands were made strong by the hands of the Mighty *God* of Jacob (From there *is* the Shepherd, the Stone of Israel) (Genesis 49:24).

Chapter 67

Thank You, Ma'am–You're Welcome, Sir

That has a nice ring to it, don't you think? The way we speak to each other sets the tone and paves the way for delightful and relational conversation. It's a hurry-up-get-busy world we live in today. We no sooner finish one task on our smartphone, iPad, or computer before something else pulls us away, not even allowing us to take a breath. Does our mind have any down time—ever?

Politeness seems to have gone by the wayside in our simple everyday activities. It seems we have never been so far out of touch in such a fast-paced technological world. Also, it seems a bit odd that the advancements in science would affect us this way. Our "wants" can't seem to be obtained quickly enough. This reminds me of a child saying, "I want it, and I want it now!" We learned during childhood about breaking that nasty habit, guess it would serve us well to take another look at respective attitudes. Nowadays a helpful required subject in school might be called, "The Art of Respect." It would open up a whole new world of ages past.

How do I respond when I encounter rudeness? On my best days, I can usually get an ill-tempered individual to attain a place of humor, encouragement, or at least a pleasant state of mind. On my worst days, I tend to make them wish they had already achieved a better frame of mind before I get to them. I'm being honest with you; I am as imperfect as anyone. If I'm in a "hot-under-the-collar" mood, I might not leave the situation in a better state than when I got there. And by the way that is not Christlike when I add my rudeness. With that being said, I must then go apologize for my behavior without a "but" at the end of the sentence. It's important to not use an apology as an excuse. I am happy to say, I rarely create a crime scene I need to return to.

Thinking beforehand about what an objectionable person might be going through is an excellent diffuser as we apply kindness and consideration. I call this responding in the opposite spirit. Try it! In an ideal world, we would all practice drinking from this wellspring of thoughtfulness on a more regular basis. Showing you care is extremely rewarding and makes a huge difference in a person's life and what they do the rest of the day. Sometimes we just need to remember that none of us is without frustrating days. I learned a long time ago that it can't always be the other person that's the problem. Actually, that finally sunk in one day as I was looking in a mirror while I was very upset. I guess I wanted to admire how mad I was as it seemed to help me plan what I was going to do about it! The Lord spoke to my heart and said "Denise, it can't always be someone else's fault. Look at yourself." Ouch!

Remember that Golden Rule we learned as children? I find we often fail to remember the simplest things that make such enormous differences.

> Do to others whatever you would like them to do to you. This is the essence of all that is taught in the law and the prophets (Matthew 7:12 NLT).

> Do not seek revenge or bear a grudge against a fellow Israelite, but love your neighbor as yourself. I am the LORD (Leviticus 19:18 NLT).

Chapter 68

Precious Cargo

It's time to ship a package; it could be a birthday, anniversary, Christmas, or a "just because." However the package takes the voyage—by air or land—we always take the best possible care preparing it for the trip. It's fragile, so there's insurance we can purchase in case of a mishap, like getting damaged or lost, and it gives us peace of mind in most situations. But what if it's irreplaceable? I've shipped countless items which are irreplaceable because of sentimental value and cannot be duplicated. It's risky, and I knew it as soon as I handed it over to the carrier, but off it goes with a hope and a prayer for the best arrival.

Sentimentality is a comforting frame of mind that nearly everyone cozies up to now and then. On a scale of one to ten, I'm a fifteen! My home is rather eclectic because of that big 'ol number 15. I have difficulty at times choosing what I don't like, because I see most everything in its own particular distinctiveness. There are a few other members in my family that are sentimental buffs, so I send oodles of precious cargo to them. It's meaningful to them, and they want to pass it on to their children, or so they tell me.

This sentimentality brings several things to mind. For instance, how do you think we should package or care for our youngsters when we send them on **their** way? We clothe them warmly in winter so they won't get sick. Summertime, we're ready for fun under the sun, not forgetting sunblock for fragile skin. We teach them a variety of age-appropriate skills so they are prepared for all kinds of occurrences. Come to grips early on with these ideals, because you will omit many bits and pieces. You can try telling them later on they were on a "need-to-know" basis and they weren't to that point yet. Maybe they'll buy that. I think I prayed daily for God to cover my shortcomings.

In an instruction-laden upbringing, there's one thing we may forget from time to time. Do we know how to appreciate our children's gifts? I think of my son, who is gifted with both his father's and my personality. There's nothing like looking at a youthful reflection of yourself in your offspring combined with that of a younger personality of your spouse. I have often communicated to my husband that our son is simply a younger and more powerful "you and me." If both of our personalities are combined in our son, and indeed they are, we observed early on the new blend of personality that had been created. Surely, this is evidence that God has a sense of humor and wasn't finished with our own maturity even though we became parents.

God broke the mold when He created each of us. We are fragile like a breath of wind. Our gifts are extraordinarily unique to each of us. Nurture your gifts so they can edify and make sure your cargo is ready for shipping. Pass on the treasures of God that are inside your children and to their children's children.

> Teach them to your children. Talk about them when you are at home and when you are on the road, when you are going to bed and when you are getting up (Deuteronomy 11:19 NLT).

> That the man of God may be complete, thoroughly equipped for every good work (2 Timothy 3:17).

Chapter 69

No Problem, I'll Do That Later

Sound familiar? This page may as well been left blank right after the title to make a point. Each of us probably has something that comes immediately to mind of what we should be about. The culprit is procrastination. It's one of the biggest joy zappers I can think of. If we could only ask this question in a timely manner: "Is what I am about to delay going to bring a positive result in any way?" Instead, we make a comment like, "Why do now what I can surely do later; after all, there's plenty of time?"

That sounds manageable, but in fact it's utter deception. We only think we have plenty of time. Unlike God's timeframe, our clock operates in human time. Twenty-four hours for us is definitely not as a thousand years. That's why our lives are of such significance to God. He set our clocks in motion and promised to always be at our side, helping us make the best of our ever-so-brief time here on earth. Let's live our lives so that it's our heart's desire for each other as well. There is no better way to show our love for God than loving others.

As I mention throughout this book, *Kairos Moments*, I am no better than anyone else; different, yes, but no better. I've spoken the following phrases upon many occasions and live to tell the horror of it:

- I'll call later.
- I'll come by and see you tomorrow.
- No worries, I'll finish that chore later
- Deliver the welcome package later.
- Make the hospital visit later.
- Meet with a friend later.
- Plan a special date for my spouse later.
- Chat with my child later.
- Apologize later.
- Take a class later.
- Say I love you later.

The list goes on and on. A tough question is, "Have you come to know that "later" never had a chance to be your opportunity?" As I write those last few words, I will simply say, I've learned the lesson of not saying, "I love you" enough. I have missed more opportunities than I would like to remember when I did not do what God was asking me to do in meeting the need of someone else. I dismissed it as though such a necessity would wait to fit my schedule. The few opportunities listed above are enough to make me stop and reprioritize my time schedule on a daily basis. How about you?

Regret is a relative to procrastination. Think of it. Procrastination is the firstborn and regret is the sibling that follows. We think we're achieving more time by putting things off, but actually we're making a "to do" list that cannot be completed. The seed of regret has been planted. What usually happens is that we cross something off our list of things to do which is vital to someone else. That alone should be one of the most important positions to take; thinking about someone else. This, of course, is not to devalue our own responsibilities, but think of others as just as important. I find that when I reevaluate my wants and desires, there is an allowance for the essentials of others to take the forefront position of consideration in my mind, as well as in my heart. I really do want to be a Good Samaritan, don't you?

I think sometimes we pass the blame as to why we didn't "do something," justifying our lack of action. This leaves us with the realization we alone are greatly responsible for the consequences and our inadequacies. Regret fills our minds with "what if's?" Be mindful that no one person is responsible for doing all things, and that's how it is supposed to be. What we don't or can't do is an assignment or responsibility for others to accomplish. I wish I could be more like my husband. He can multi-task with the best of them. I can't pour coffee and talk at the same time. But I'm passionate about that one thing at a time I'm doing!

We are wonderfully made. If God authorizes you to do something, He is responsible for showing you how to get it done. Finishing one thing well is how you begin the next.

> But, beloved, do not forget this one thing, that with the Lord one day is as a thousand years, and a thousand years as one day (2 Peter 3:8).

But a certain Samaritan, as he journeyed, came where he was. And when he saw him, he had compassion (Luke 10:33).

And be kind to one another, tenderhearted, forgiving one another, even as God in Christ forgave you (Ephesians 4:32).

Chapter 70

Drat Those Bad Habits!

It takes 30 days to stop a bad habit. Great, you're going to change things up. However, there's one significant step. You have to begin a new *good* habit to replace the old one. It's important to think the process through; otherwise, there's not much progress. Becoming overly focused on ending a bad habit, we may fail to realize we're at a standstill. You've stopped the one thing, but what to do instead has not occurred to you. This makes for a never-ending battle of sorts, because we are accomplishing only half the task.

Anyone can develop bad habits. A category of people that come to mind are experienced athletes. Sometimes, performance seems to be less than normal, but they can't quite put their finger on it. Today's technology lends itself well to reviewing live performances, allowing discovery of the glitch taking the athlete quite by surprise. In the sports arena, it's easy to view an athlete's mistakes, because colossal amounts of recorded games are saved for the coach's review. We may not be a professional, but personal review with sincere humility is a way to keep such things from sneaking up on us.

How many of us walk around with an entourage? Filming everyday people in everyday life isn't something any of us would probably welcome. This might be viewed as an invasion of privacy, but imagine if it could happen and consider God your coach. The moment you wake up in the morning and your Coach says "action!" The recording begins as we go about our typical day, interacting among others in the workplace, school, mall, grocery store, church, or home. The day's a wrap and film at 11. You won't be the only one watching!

I've had some bad habits for a long time and failed to notice some of them. Becoming aware, I was thankful to be enlightened of my erroneous ways. However, everyone cannot be your accountability partner; some don't care how you behave and others don't know how to approach you. Those who love me most are the ones I'm counting on and who have earned the place in my life to speak truth to me. Sure, truth hurts sometimes, but we can't deny wearing the shoe when it fits so well.

Clean house. Get rid of pesky, irritating behavior. More important, replace what's been cleaned out with a more endearing, relevant, and compatible essence of Christ.

> When an unclean spirit goes out of a man, he goes through dry places, seeking rest, and finds none. Then he says, "I will return to my house from which I came." And when he comes, he finds *it* empty, swept, and put in order. Then he goes and takes with him seven other spirits more wicked than himself, and they enter and dwell there; and the last state of that man is worse than the first (Matthew 12:43-45).

> That the LORD your God may show us the way in which we should walk and the thing we should do (Jeremiah 42:3).

> These *are* the things you shall do: Speak each man the truth to his neighbor; give judgment in your gates for truth, justice, and peace (Zechariah 8:16).

Chapter 71

Knock Knock

Knock knock. Who's there? Friend or foe? Good question because we don't run to the door with excitement these days. When there's a knock or the doorbell rings, we tend to turn the lights out or make a mad dash to another room. Sadly, today we're more cautious. I do long for the day when neighbors were welcome to stop by without notice for a visit or ask for a helping hand. Folks used to stop by to borrow a cup of sugar, or nowadays an extra jar of spaghetti sauce for a hungry family and a hurried mom. I refuse to believe those days are gone forever, but that's just me. Everyone's association with us may not always be in our best interest, but I continue to hope in all things.

The same goes for us spiritually. Discernment is a key factor when answering our front door these days. We don't know who's at the door unless we take a peek. Similarly, we must be discerning about our daily routine and what consumes our thoughts. How we wait upon the Lord for answers and direction will determine who comes to visit. Women especially are beings with extremely enthusiastic minds! We seriously have to think about our thoughts. Guilt and condemnation are two visitors who show up much too often without being invited. Productive waiting consists of securing thoughts from God and rejecting lies from the Enemy. Purposefully, invite self-control for good company.

Typically, we all believe it when God sets us free from an assortment of conditions that previously felt like weights on our shoulders. The stumbling block comes when we wait impatiently. Trust in God is indeed the freedom that is adequate to keep us from allowing back in a past laden with guilt. Engaging our own thoughts is beneficial. Listening like one being taught gives us staying power necessary to ascertain God's leading in preparation to hear.

Use the peephole; don't willingly open the door because you're curious! Sit still in your overstuffed chair enjoying the fact that your past is your past. Remind yourself that no longer are the weights on your shoulders nearly as heavy preventing victory! Do not miss an opportunity to increase your trust in God and believe that you are who He says you are. To be encouraged, realize you are not yet where you are going, but you are certainly not where you used to be.

> If any of you lacks wisdom, let him ask of God, who gives to all liberally and without reproach, and it will be given to him (James 1:5).

> *Is* not your reverence your confidence? And the integrity of your ways your hope? (Job 4:6).

> Therefore if the Son makes you free, you shall be free indeed (John 8:36).

> Not boasting of things beyond measure, *that is*, in other men's labors, but having hope, *that* as your faith is increased, we shall be greatly enlarged by you in our sphere (2 Corinthians 10:15).

Chapter 72

The Butterfly

What's the first thing you notice when you watch a butterfly flutter by? Do you immediately remember the caterpillar it used to be? When I observe a butterfly, I declare its stunning and natural beauty instantly. I take in its elaborate color, intricate design, and grace of its delicate wings as it floats upon the wind with seemingly little effort. As the butterfly is drawn to the sweet nectar of flowers, I find myself whimsically wishing I were a flower! I stand as still as possible, hoping one may light upon me so I might further observe its complex beauty. Then once again it flutters away to do what butterflies do.

Though a butterfly is one of God's many amazing creations, even more so, we desire people to be drawn to us! Is it because of our outward or inner beauty that we desire others to be drawn to us? Answer truthfully. We present ourselves as best we can with what we have. We may be attracted to someone that is striking in one way or another. But unlike the butterfly, it is our inner beauty that will outlast any outer display of attractiveness we exhibit. Inside is where lasting change takes place.

We are unable to see the transformation from caterpillar to butterfly, and it is extraordinary. After the caterpillar has prepared its cocoon, that's where it instinctively knows it needs to stay until it emerges completely changed. It's vital for the butterfly to maintain this temporary habitat in order to make use of its new strength and complete transformation.

This metamorphosis can teach us about numerous seasons of our lives. Before a change takes place, there has to be a season of transformation—like in the quiet dead of winter when most trees are leafless. The appearance is that nothing is happening. But below the surface, there is a new blending of vitality and splendor.

Quiet times are more significant than we may realize.

When the Lord quiets you, it doesn't mean He has abandoned you. To the contrary, He is beginning a transformation within you so that you will emerge changed. We don't see the butterfly as what it was—a caterpillar. We see what it is now. The butterfly never returns to the cocoon to change back into a caterpillar, nor is it God's plan for us to return back to what we were before the transformation. God is never too late and never too early with His plans. Trust that God is doing a great work in you even if it appears to be motionless. Whatever change is being done in you, be ready for others to be drawn to you because you display outwardly what's been done inwardly. You will be seen as the individual you are now, not what you were. Before you know it, you will be off to do what it is you do.

> And do not be conformed to this world, but be trans-formed by the renewing of your mind, that you may prove what *is* that good and acceptable and perfect will of God (Romans 12:2).

> But we all, with unveiled face, beholding as in a mirror the glory of the Lord, are being transformed into the same image from glory to glory, just as by the Spirit of the Lord (2 Corinthians 3:18).

> When I was a child, I talked like a child, I thought like a child, I reasoned like a child. When I became a man, I put the ways of childhood behind me (1 Corinthians 13:11 NIV).

Chapter 73

Doubt Is Not Believable

I believed the situation was resolved. But then doubt came. At one time or another, I think we all experience a wedge of doubt that crosses the threshold of our minds and plans. We can be blindsided by an unexpected blow to our faith. On any given day, I encounter someone who is on the verge of losing a grip on what the unchanging Word says. Trading in belief for doubt is definitely not trading up. Apprehension closes the window of possibilities and the hope that's available in all things. It's like we can see through the glass of the window, but we can no longer get beyond the wall that holds the window. I believe that is hope calling to us. It's at that moment we choose to trust God's promises that He helps us in our unbelief. In Mark 9:24, we read, "Immediately the father of the child cried out and said with tears, 'Lord, I believe; help my unbelief!'" I have included this scripture right here, because that's how quickly we need to grasp it. We can then move forward with what we began to do before doubt crept in.

What does God do with that moment of belief, no matter how brief it may be? I think it has value in our personal "belief bank." Should we discount that moment of hope? Absolutely not! Take a look at Matthew 14:27-33. Jesus says not to be afraid and to recognize who He is. Jesus gives a command to Peter, and he begins walking on the water. Then he was distracted and became afraid because he saw the effects of the wind. Jesus reached out and caught Peter. Jesus asked, Why did you doubt, Peter? Seeing this, those on the boat worshiped Jesus and believed He was the Son of God. In that moment of belief there was fruit.

Uncertainties need not win and reign over our lives. Belief the size of a mustard seed of faith is victorious! We beat ourselves up with doubt, a tool of the Enemy, instead of enriching our minds with credence. Consider the moment in time between assurance and skepticism. Now, consider what time is to God. He is timeless. The Bible says: "With the Lord one day is as a thousand years, and a thousand years as one day" (2 Peter 3:8). God created time for our benefit. Is a moment of certainty worth only a few seconds in our minds, or is it worth a thousand years in God's time? There is greater value than we comprehend in our belief, even if it is only a mere moment. Any measure of one's creed is what we have to grasp in order to strengthen our faith. Think of David as he faced Goliath. The Word tells us he RAN toward him. I think he ran because he knew what doubt would do if he thought about it too long.

> Now faith is the substance of things hoped for, the evidence of things not seen (Hebrews 11:1).

> You *are* My witnesses, says the LORD, "And My servant whom I have chosen, that you may know and believe Me, and understand that I *am* He. Before Me there was no God formed, nor shall there be after Me" (Isaiah 43:10).

> For assuredly, I say to you, whoever says to this mountain, "Be removed and be cast into the sea," and does not doubt in his heart, but believes that those things he says will be done, he will have whatever he says (Mark 11:23).

Chapter 74

Me? Lazy?

ays come and go, and so does my desire to be productive. Not all the time, but there are definitely sprinklings here and there. I think most of us experience lazy days now and then. Personalities have much to do with it. I have a friend who decides what day she is going to do "nothing" and puts it on the calendar. That way is too structured for me, and it doesn't make sense, to me anyway. I mean, how do I know I will want to do nothing on say, Tuesday? What if I do want to do something? Then there's pressure to NOT do anything! Whew!!

I'm more of a free spirit moved by spontaneity. It's very exciting, but there have been times when I would sure like to have been a bit more of a planner. Over the years, there has been evidence that some scheduling would have benefited my family and me. Being a work in progress, I've made adjustments and found my calendar has plenty of blank spaces to satisfy my flexibility and spontaneity. I've learned to appreciate my gifts.

My best friend and I are graciously the opposite. She is V-E-R-Y organized. She can't stop organizing. You might be surprised to know that we have the best possible relationship. Over the years, she has become more outgoing, flexible, tries new ideas, and even likes sparkly things. I, on the other hand, have become a bit more restricted, organized, enjoy a routine, and appreciate simplicity.

The one vital commonality we share is our love for Christ. We sharpen each other like iron sharpens iron because of His authority. We hold each other accountable for things that really matter. We lock arms and go the distance, whatever it takes, which speaks to me about unity. I am forever hopeful that all of us can learn to work together with every one of our zany differences. I say zany because to one person another's gift may seem useless, confusing, ridiculous, silly, too relaxed, too hard pressed, or too outdated in the world's latest technology. Some gifts we simply can't seem to wrap our minds around.

Have you found yourself questioning how someone else gets things done? I have; my husband. There is no greater difference than a man and a woman; how they think, how they relate, and how they solve problems. It's by no coincidence that my husband questions how I do things either. It was not by some haphazard idea that God made us poles apart. His way defines the bigger picture of relationship. If we want to get along and be productive, we must discover the benefits in each other's way of doing things. We can learn from each other without losing the personality God created in each of us. If you have a tendency to have too many lazy days; with nothing to show at the end of the day, observe someone else's gift to embrace each task to completion. If you have a tendency to do your job *and* everyone else's, take a look at someone who has learned *not* to do that!

> The way of the lazy *man is* like a hedge of thorns, But the way of the upright *is* a highway (Proverbs 15:19).

> As iron sharpens iron, so a man sharpens the countenance of his friend (Proverbs 27:17).

> Having then gifts differing according to the grace that is given to us, *let us use them*: if prophecy, *let us prophesy* in proportion to our faith or ministry, *let us use* it in our ministering; he who teaches, in teaching; he who exhorts, in exhortation; he who gives, with liberality; he who leads, with diligence; he who shows mercy, with cheerfulness (Romans 12:6-8).

Chapter 75

Does the Fire Really Need Another Log?

When it comes to disagreements, emotion can run high, and if there's any rationale present it seems to vacate the premises. This attitude, when in attendance, has the propensity to "fuel the fire" of an opponent. How should we best deal with these situations? Lashing out and retaliating are a couple of ways. But those tend to be reactional retorts instead of responses that neutralize. Each person thinking their way is correct presses in to persuade the other into agreement. All we've done is merely thrown another log on the fire, and it begins to blaze. Unable to solve a discrepancy, both parties reach an impasse as the temperature rises. Things always worsen when the Enemy sets a fire ablaze. Where does that go, except in a big circle like thieves with torches surrounding a band of wagons, similar to a scene from a Western movie? The attack is on. Wrongdoings and faultfindings are shot like arrows of division resulting in harm, anger, and unforgiveness which cause many people to be unapproachable in the future. The fire continues to smolder in many cases.

Once I learned the method of responding in the opposite spirit, I put it into practice. It works! This method is an effective tool. Deep soul-searching, along with years of experience, helped me determine that this step is prerequisite when experiencing opposition. If we want to alter a result, we need to respond differently. Even if our way or thought is correct, we have to find a way to express it. Unearth a kind word first. Everyone needs validation, and it's an effective diffuser. Is there a point of goodwill on either side? Surely there is one. But to find it and really see it, we must get out of our own way. Covering our eyes is often a way to choose blindness. We don't know how to see the good in something else; therefore, we would rather double down in being right no matter what.

The opposite spirit is exactly what it sounds like. Respond in a way that is the opposite of let's say, anger, because that's a biggie. The effect is usually immediate and evident on the face of the person you are addressing. Someone has to take the first step. God has asked me more than once: "Why shouldn't it be you, Denise?" Yes, it's a hard pill to swallow, but once you've done it, you feel better. It's like taking bad-tasting medicine. No one really wants to take it, but we know there will be good results. This is pleasing to God, because it takes everyone to a productive level of communication. Instead of starting a fire, learn how to extinguish one.

Take time to reflect on what James and John asked Jesus when He was not received well in a village of the Samaritans.

> And when His disciples James and John saw *this,* they said, "Lord, do You want us to command fire to come down from heaven and consume them, just as Elijah did?" But He turned and rebuked them, and said, "You do not know what manner of spirit you are of" (Luke 9:54-55).

> Live in harmony with one another; do not be haughty (snobbish, high-minded, exclusive), but readily adjust yourself to [people, things] *and* give yourselves to humble tasks. Never overestimate yourself *or* be wise in your own conceits (Romans 12:16 AMPC).

Chapter 76

Clandestine: My Secret Place

The only one who truly knows me is God. He can give me one hundred percent of His attention one hundred percent of the time. Wherever I am or whatever I am doing, He will convene with me. God is not duty-bound by obligation and is always available. I am with Him in my "Secret Place."

The morning is awakening—that peaceful time just before sunrise. The sun's light is beginning to upstage the trees across the yard from my living room. Leaves rustle as tiny creatures scamper about. Soon after, the clouds reflect the sun and a myriad of rainbow colors float across the horizon. A cup of coffee in hand and the aroma of scented candles fill the air; I appreciate the tranquil time, no matter how brief. Sitting in my big comfy chair is only one of my many secret places to pray and contemplate. It's one I can enjoy before greeting the world outside my door.

That last paragraph sounded surreal didn't it? Yes, the peacefulness of the dewy fresh morning air and the quiet of my personal castle I call home. That's my life now, but it wasn't always so when my son was little. Many times, I made the drive to grammar school in my PJs to deliver my son, but then who hasn't. I made sure to own a bathrobe that was presentable. We moms of little ones were happy to greet one another in the parking lot, and without a breath of judgment. I was on a different clock in those days, and my praying time was on the drive back home. Sound familiar?

Our busyness encapsulates us all too quickly. Many of us today miss the opportunity to spend quiet time with our "heavenly Planner." Often, we turn to our "Daily Planner" instead; men and women alike. We say; oh just one more thing before I connect with a devotional mindset; besides there's always tomorrow, and I simply have too much to do right now. Unfortunately, some of us put off visiting our secret place, because we don't have any major disasters and think "I'm good." The question is; "For how long?" Putting off things of vital significance invites chaos.

My husband has had opportunities to teach sales seminars; he understood the relevance of preparation. He reiterated the "7-Ps of Planning— "Proper, Prior, Planning, Prevents, Pitiful, Poor, Performance"—at every staff sales meeting in his own business. Procrastination is NOT one of the 7-Ps. Our sixteenth president, Abraham Lincoln, said it like this: "Give me six hours to chop down a tree, and I will spend the first four sharpening the axe." Seek excellence, before you start your day. Perhaps Jesus said it best in the following verse.

> [Martha] had a sister called Mary, who also sat at Jesus' feet and heard His word. But Martha was distracted with much serving, and she approached Him and said, "Lord, do You not care that my sister has left me to serve alone? Therefore tell her to help me." Jesus answered and said to her, "Martha, Martha, you are worried and troubled about many things. But one thing is needed, and Mary has chosen that good part, which will not be taken away from her" (Luke 10:38-43).

> But you, when you pray, go into your room, and when you have shut your door, pray to your Father who *is* in the secret *place*; and your Father who sees in secret will reward you openly (Matthew 6:6).

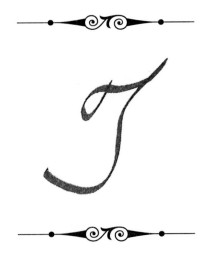

Chapter 77

Masterpiece

Doing right by our fellowman could be considered a form of art. There is an amount of humble beauty in every person. In a manner of speaking, we are born as a blank canvas. We stand ready to become like a full-size person emerging from a pop-up book embellished with a vibrancy of color. How we treat someone should be a reflection of how we want to be treated. Caring for our fellowman in love is the Greatest Commandment given us by Christ. The fruit thereof is the beauty of all mankind. We are all masterpieces and should be handled with essential care—care that causes us to proliferate. God certainly must experience new joy each time He creates a masterpiece. His details, as he paints my life, are more than I can begin to comprehend. Many artists birth in their minds what they desire to paint before taking brush in hand. They are driven to put it on canvas. This is how God saw us before we were conceived, completely and wonderfully made.

As young children, we are mentally shaped and molded by the words and actions of those caring for us. Our lives flow from one period of time to the next as we journey onward. All of us navigate monumental roads enduring countless and sorted alterations. Some are fast-paced like the Autobahn in Germany, and some are slow-paced like an uphill twisting road. We take on different looks, acquire various strengths, display intricate personalities, and acquire bumps and bruises, even developing callused edges.

When the gentle hand of an artist picks up an artifact in disrepair, the befitting thing is to begin the process of restoration. I am hopeful that mankind will always be moved to embolden someone who is heavily yoked by the hardships of life. Everything is beautiful in its time, but sometimes we lose sight of that truth. I'm comforted to know that all of us can call upon the ultimate Artist, the Potter himself, who formed us and transforms us.

An artifact needs to be found, however, before the complete restoration process can begin. This procedure, although challenging, can bring the piece to its original and magnificent origin. Of course, there is unbridled elation with the discovery of any rare and fragile treasure. Contrary to an artifact, however, we of God's design have to continually seek and find Him. It is never God who loses us and it is never Him who authors our pitfalls. All we need to do is ask, and He awaits us with anticipation. This is what splendidly sets us apart from anything manmade. We were fashioned *an original* by the Potter himself.

> All things were made through Him, and without Him nothing was made that was made (John 1:3).

> I will praise You, for I am fearfully *and* wonderfully made; marvelous are Your works, and *that* my soul knows very well (Psalm 139:14).

> For You did form my inward parts; You did knit me together in my mother's womb (Psalm 139:13 AMPC).

> Who being the brightness of *His* glory and the express image of His person, and upholding all things by the word of His power, when He had by Himself purged our sins, sat down at the right hand of the Majesty on high (Hebrews 1:3).

Chapter 78

Three Hearts

God has given us each a heart, and I believe we experience the fullness of what it means to have one. It's much more than what makes us "tick." It means to me, that we each find ourselves experiencing the full range of all aspects regarding the spiritual heart from joy to sorrow. There are hurt hearts, hardened hearts, and most important, liberated hearts.

The hurting heart has experienced the impact of a situation. The hardened heart is an impenetrable heart. The heart we hopefully yearn to know is the liberating heart—the willingness to let go of something and willingly take a risk again for the sake of love.

It goes without saying, we have all learned about emotional pain. One of the things I've personally learned is that God is more interested in what we do with a hurt than with the hurt itself. Not wanting us to remain in a state of pain, He cares how we get beyond what has harmed us. If we allow our heart to be hardened, it's difficult to begin anew because of carrying fragmented odds and ends of our past that can quickly add up and weigh us down. Learning to embrace a liberating heart, we can allow for freedom that enriches us as we apply His requirement of forgiveness.

What happens when we respond correctly to issues of the heart? When we are hurt, we are able to let go of the offense. If our heart is hardened, we are able to lay pride aside and see with clarity. As we liberate what is breaking our hearts, we are able to love freely again. Disobedience causes insecurity rather than security. There is great value in being able to recognize disobedience for what it really is.

> These things I have spoken to you, that in Me you may have peace. In the world you will have tribulation; but be of good cheer, I have overcome the world (John 16:33).

> A merry heart makes a cheerful countenance, but by sorrow of the heart the spirit is broken (Proverbs 15:13).

God is wise in *heart* and *mighty in strength*. Who has hardened *himself* against Him and prospered? (Job 9:4).

In Him we have redemption through His blood, the forgiveness of sins, according to the riches of His grace (Ephesians 1:7).

Even if they sin against you seven times in a day and seven times come back to you saying "I repent," you must forgive them (Luke 17:4 NIV).

For as by one man's disobedience many were made sinners, so also by one Man's obedience many will be made righteous (Romans 5:19).

Chapter 79

I Want It, Or Do I?

This is how we are—want, want, and want. Not only that, but we want it now! I know this isn't everyone in a nutshell; but now and then I've found myself in this category. We often wonder where mine is; whether it is a job, promotion, financial freedom, position in ministry, friends, influence, reward, or validation. Well, it's on the way, "if." This is the kicker; "if" we are reliable. That's part of responsibility. Oh, but we don't want THAT! We just want the "stuff." Not striving to be reliable could mean we lack the desire to perform our responsibilities with integrity and heart. Parading around as though we have it all together is likely our strategy. For what? The title? Yes, primarily when we're "feeling" that we're all about ourselves.

If this is our attitude, I would suggest it's time to explore the mirror challenge. Take a long, direct, and honest surveillance of what you see. I know it might sound weird, but begin to speak out loud with prayer-like countenance asking what you stand for. You're not looking at your face to notice your physical appearance, but in fact, see way beyond what you look like. This can be difficult to do, but remember, God is right there with you to keep your thoughts in His direction.

My precious son, when he was little used the word "need" more often than "want." He not only wanted something, but he also said so with strong facial expression, intent on getting it, and a fervent voice with the words "I *need*" it, whatever it might have been. I asked, do you simply want it, or do you have a real need? We had many discussions about the difference between "want" and "need." Not to my surprise after our dialogue, he said: "Okay, Mommy, I neeeeeeeed it." More conversations would follow. As of this writing, he is 23 years old, in college, and I find myself with respect and love, still having those discerning conversations occasionally.

We are each a "movement" in our personal timeline. Do we want to be an enthralling movement—one that is riveting, action-packed, and makes a difference? Attaining goals such as that are only accomplished by laying down pride, having a mind that continues to learn, and is being vulnerable to God. Also, being transparent and accountable helps answer the question—Do I truly want it?

Firstly, I say it like this: I want everything the Bible says *I can have,* and I want to be everything the Bible says *I can be.* Obviously, none of us is capable of being ALL of everything, but I have the mindset that God likes us to ask for our needs. He will give us His measure, and actually in many realms, I believe He has already given us our measure. We've simply disbursed and developed incorrectly in many areas. Secondly, but just as important, I say; I don't want anything that His Word says *I should not have* or be anything I *should not be.* What we don't accomplish is not a bad thing, because it takes all of us to be the whole Church in Christ's eyes.

One problem is coveting what someone else has. Our natural abilities are capable of this to such a degree it's done so at times with guile. We might even be willing to use deceitfulness to keep someone from having what they've achieved. Sure, we see where they are, but we don't see how they got there; and those are important ingredients. It's like baking bread without yeast. It's NOT going to rise, no matter what we do to convince the bread, it simply won't rise without the correct ingredients to make it do so. We cannot get what we want if we aren't willing to go through the process that gets us there. Those are the defining snippets. Everything matters.

> No servant can serve two masters; for either he will hate the one and love the other, or else he will be loyal to the one and despise the other. You cannot serve God and mammon (Luke 16:13).

> Not that I speak in regard to need, for I have learned in whatever state I am, to be content: I know how to be abased, and I know how to abound. Everywhere and in all things I have learned both to be full and to be hungry, both to abound and to suffer need. I can do all things through Christ who strengthens me (Philippians 4:11-13).

> But in all *things* we commend ourselves as ministers of God: in much patience, in tribulations, in needs, in distresses (2 Corinthians 6:4).

Chapter 80

Attention Is Seasonal

Among sibling rivalry, it only seems like a brother or sister is getting more attention at a given moment. If you parent a large family or have a blended family, this is more than likely a very true statement for you. This goes not only for the home, but describes growing pains of some churches.

Christians like to think they have it all together, but it seems there is also sibling rivalry when a church experiences growth. If you're experiencing it, the new campus addition or annex may be considered the "baby," even if it starts out much larger either in number of people or campus site. It has the appearance of being well established, fully operational, and tremendous leadership for all venues of ministry. The truth is it's a work in progress needing a lot of "parental attention." Just like a child needs to sit on a parent's lap sometimes for comfort and reassurance, a new church campus or enterprise needs extra attention from time to time. A youngster ventures farther each time leaving mom's side becoming more acquainted with strengths and abilities before returning to "home base" or square one for safety. No one feels safe or adequate when experiencing an awkward stage of growth. Extra attention is what overcomes hurdles.

My best friend and I experienced an awkward, but wonderful, season together with our sons who are only months apart in age. We did almost everything together. Her son was extremely tall, and our son was considerably smaller for his age (not anymore!). Both being verbally expressive, there was usually no need to speak for them except when people didn't believe they were the same age. You've seen a puppy with big feet; well my friend's son was like that! She was helping him learn to roller skate at a school party and, oh my goodness, she had her hands full, even though she is pretty strong. He tried and tried until he learned to maneuver those feet which earned him a big smile on his face that he gladly traded for the ache of defeat on his bum. On vacation, we always had to take the boys' birth certificates for daily activities! Restaurants wanted to give one a children's menu while the other wouldn't get one and was frowned at if he insisted! Waiting in line at Disneyland, one was offered a snack, and the other wasn't. The looks on their faces were priceless while under adult scrutiny. It became ritualistic to clarify they were the same age and they always "had each other's back."

Then, one day everything changed. Growing pains were awkward and hurtful at times, but perseverance paid off. So whether you're a parent of siblings during an awkward stage, or experiencing supernatural growth in your church or business, remember to give seasonal attention as needed. It's amazing what can be done when we get the vision, rather than using a time clock to judge how long something is taking.

> You water its ridges abundantly, You settle its furrows; You make it soft with showers, You bless its growth (Psalm 65:10).

> From whom the whole body, joined and knit together by what every joint supplies, according to the effective working by which every part does its share, causes growth of the body for the edifying of itself in love (Ephesians 4:16).

Chapter 81

Dig Deep and Uproot Those Weeds

My husband enjoys mowing the lawn, and afterward it looks fresh and manicured. The following morning, I like to take another look at how nice it looks. Hmmmmph! Almost without fail, there they are. Those dandelions have popped up overnight! Mowing the lawn made the yard look nice, but mowing alone won't get rid of weeds. It takes a shovel to get down to the root and remove it, or you must use weed killer. I prefer weed killer. Our yard is much smaller here in Tennessee compared to our home in Oregon where we needed a tractor! At that time, I wasn't concerned about the dandelions as much as I was the wild blackberries that would overtake everything, like kudzu does here in the Smoky Mountains of Tennessee. The point is: You have to get down to the root of things sometimes.

We cannot treat surface symptoms and expect to take care of a problem. Would a bandage fix a broken arm or leg? Not even a hundred bandages would do that. We must get below the surface to do the work. Once that's done, the rehabilitation process begins. Many precious people are walking around looking well-manicured on the outside, but they are in terrific pain on the inside. I want to help them because there is so much God wants to do for them, in them, and through them. Removing weeds that strangle allows a person to flourish with the springing forth of fruit from roots of good and healthy seed.

Pertaining to our spiritual walk, we must "reteach" below the surface of our outer flesh. These are issues of the heart. The surface area only goes so deep, then it is no longer the surface, but the "deep," wherein lies the challenge. When a person has been operating with a particular method for a long time, this can be a difficult ordeal. I've always heard it is easier to teach from a clean slate than reteach someone. I've found in some instances this is true.

It's like clothes we wear to enhance the good things about our appearance while concealing the mess underneath. Okay, not everyone, but you know who you are, and I'm there with you. We keep wearing what hides imperfections while ignoring what we could do to improve the underneath.

Simply saying "Yuk!" only seems like a good solution. Turning away from a mirror or reflection of ourselves in a window, we may choose to cover up what we don't like, ignore it and just move on. Because heaven knows there is always something being marketed to make it easy for us to continue this facade!

To fix underlying problems or potential plight, we need the whole foundational teaching of the Word, from Genesis to Revelation, nothing omitted and nothing added. Cutting corners, applying bandages, or using a mere patch is nothing more than a quick-fix and that means trouble in the making.

I like using visuals, so next time you see a construction site for a high-rise building, take a look at the depth of its foundation. When living in Oregon, we enjoyed visiting the city of Portland for the weekend and made the most of it by staying right downtown in the middle of such a beautiful city. From our hotel, we watched the progress of a tower being built during our visits over a period of about a year. The deeply dug out portion for the foundation was not aesthetically pleasing and certainly didn't hold a candle to the finished structure. But without stability, the skyscraper would be like us trying to balance or stand on unstable ground. Without a strong foundation, it is difficult for anything to last very long.

In every man, there is a glimmer of teachable hope.

> You must teach what is in accord with sound doctrine (Titus 2:1 NIV 1984).

> For a fire will be kindled by my wrath, one that burns down to the realm of the dead below. It will devour the earth and its harvests and set afire the foundations of the mountains (Deuteronomy 32:22 NIV).

> If you should say, 'How shall we persecute him?'— Since the root of the matter is found in me (Job 19:28).

Chapter 82

They ~ Them ~ Me

It's not what they say; it's not about them; nor is it about how I feel.

Our country is in need of prayer. That's an understatement, and prayer should never ever be underrated. No matter how much we are told not to pray in today's world, it is something that cannot and will not be taken from me. How about you? Prayer is not the "least we can do," rather, it's the best we can do. Prayer is an honor and a powerful force!

I run into people who often say: "They said" or "Ask them." Well, I have a question about these conversations concerning various matters: Who are the so-called "they" and "them?" Sometimes, I've noticed people don't like it when you get specific by asking. The best two questions to ask are: "Who am I?" and "Who resides in me?" Christ resides in me, and I reside in Him. That's who I want to go with. I desire to say what He says and do what He does. Please notice the word "does." Jesus is not past tense.

Who you are is a breath of fresh air, a child of God, a light in darkness to the lost and afraid, a path to victory, a voice for the voiceless, and an arm to help a fallen brother or sister. But most of all, you are a prayer warrior. No matter what your prayer sounds like, it touches the heart of God, and He assuredly hears you. If you are someone who doubts how you pray or what you sound like, please don't let that inhibit you. The Enemy would like you to believe anything contrary to the Word of God. Know that you know that you know; in a single breath, God can hear you.

Does God need our prayers for Him to be God? No. But prayer changes things in ways that your wildest imagination cannot comprehend. One of the most conclusive aspects of prayer is that it fine-tunes me and influences everything surrounding me. I especially see this to be true when I pray for an adversary in my life. Delving into prayer for an enemy will definitely help you reach a deeper level in your prayer life. For this, sometimes I have to pray for God to help me **want** to pray. A word spoken in prayer is the release and outpouring of hope and God's best for mankind. God does not show partiality among men as it says in Romans 2:11: "For there is no partiality with God."

Your voice and your prayers matter a great deal; especially for the leadership of our country. You might think, *How can my little prayer matter to any government seat, office, or school administration? How can one voice matter?* It matters because God's Word says in Psalm 77:1 that when you cry out to Him with your voice, He will give His ear to you. That's a comforting truth. No matter where you are or what's happening in your life, He is always in your personal space.

> For unto us a Child is born, unto us a Son is given; and the government will be upon His shoulder. And His name will be called Wonderful, Counselor, Mighty God, Everlasting Father, Prince of Peace (Isaiah 9:6).

> You are of God, little children, and have overcome them, because He who is in you is greater than he who is in the world (1 John 4:4).

> He said to them, "But who do you say that I am?" Peter answered and said to Him, "You are the Christ." (Mark 8:29).

> For I through the law died to the law that I might live to God. I have been crucified with Christ; it is no longer I who live, but Christ lives in me; and the *life* which I now live in the flesh I live by faith in the Son of God, who loved me and gave Himself for me (Galatians 2:19-20).

Chapter 83

Inheritance

A collection of challenges ahead of us are set in motion for good reason and will be used as teaching tools. This is something I understand is true, and I will give it my all. We leave an inheritance to our children, and in doing so, the travels along these toll roads of life will be sprinkled with mistakes and grace. I don't want to give God what costs me nothing. I plant seeds of inheritance, and sometimes I do a better job than others in how I prepare the soil. When it comes to my son, I expect love to be the bearer of all in our relationship as mother and son. So what I leave as an inheritance to my son is more than what can be bought or sold. I desire to leave him possessions that will remain with him throughout his life, without exception, and then passed on to his children.

In order to leave such a vital inheritance to my son, I expect God to continually humble me by trimming my "branches" down to my very essence so new and healthy growth springs forth. I call it "trim and tuck." He trims off the dead and dried up stuff then tucks me under the shadow of His wings to heal. By our mistakes, we are able to extend grace as we teach our children, using wisdom and diplomacy. God will work with everything I am and everything I am not.

God reveals wisdom, not to make us better than others, but He allows communication with understanding for the greatest impact. We don't want our children to crumble like ceramic clay under the pressures of the world. Nor do we want them to look marvelous, but have an empty inner core that lacks vision. God is always providing us with significant opportunity, but He can also withdraw His Hand. If you ask me, that's good motivation to implement wellness into their lives instead of triggering calamity. I try to use this recipe: Praise, Pray, Acknowledge, Thanks, and Repeat. If we can look at our deepest insecurities with humility, pride will not rule us.

What does God's inheritance look like to our children? The future is not "easy street." It holds an obstacle course of its own. This may sound sad, but when I am no longer here for my son, it is my prayer he will apply good judgment instead of foolishness. In this way, he will journey hand-in-hand with the inheritance the Lord has for him. I am continually reminded there is no smaller window of time than with our children, and we can't seem to measure this precious commodity in reference to them. With every age, the time frame is unique, and I fully realize with every passing day it evaporates like water . . . almost before my very eyes.

> And again He began to teach by the sea. And a great multitude was gathered to Him, so that He got into a boat and sat *in it* on the sea; and the whole multitude was on the land facing the sea. Then He taught them many things by parables, and said to them in His teaching: "Listen! Behold, a sower went out to sow. And it happened, as he sowed, *that* some *seed* fell by the wayside; and the birds of the air came and devoured it. Some fell on stony ground, where it did not have much earth; and immediately it sprang up because it had no depth of earth. But when the sun was up it was scorched, and because it had no root it withered away. And some *seed* fell among thorns; and the thorns grew up and choked it, and it yielded no crop. But other *seed* fell on good ground and yielded a crop that sprang up, increased and produced: some thirtyfold, some sixty, and some a hundred." And He said to them, "He who has ears to hear, let him hear!"

> But when He was alone, those around Him with the twelve asked Him about the parable. And He said to them, "To you it has been given to know the mystery of the kingdom of God; but to those who are outside, all things come in parables, so that 'Seeing they may see and not perceive, and hearing they may hear and not understand; lest they should turn, and their sins be forgiven them.'"

> And He said to them, "Do you not understand this parable? How then will you understand all the parables? The sower sows the word. And these are the ones by the wayside where the word is sown. When they hear, Satan comes immediately and takes away the word that was sown in their hearts. These likewise are the ones sown on stony ground

who, when they hear the word, immediately receive it with gladness; and they have no root in themselves, and so endure only for a time. Afterward, when tribulation or persecution arises for the word's sake, immediately they stumble. Now these are the ones sown among thorns; *they are* the ones who hear the word, and the cares of this world, the deceitfulness of riches, and the desires for other things entering in choke the word, and it becomes unfruitful. But these are the ones sown on good ground, those who hear the word, accept *it*, and bear fruit: some thirtyfold, some sixty, and some a hundred" (Mark 4:1-20).

Now therefore, in the sight of all Israel, the assembly of the LORD, and in the hearing of our God, be careful to seek out all the commandments of the LORD your God, that you may possess this good land, and leave *it* as an inheritance for your children after you forever (1 Chronicles 28:8).

Then King David said to Ornan, "No, but I will surely buy *it* for the full price, for I will not take what is yours for the Lord, nor offer burnt offerings with that which costs me nothing" (1 Chronicles 21:24).

Chapter 84

Why Not Me?

Reading and praying before daylight is one of my favorite ways to benefit from my devotional time. God often speaks in the stillness of my heart as I listen. One particular morning I was thinking about people I know who are in distress from pain, injury, or some sort of suffering and hardships, which have occurred in their lives because of a set of circumstances. I have experienced such trials, and I am sure you have also. We all suffer at times. Fortunately, I stopped asking the pitiful question "Why me?" a long time ago, because God revealed to me the more pertinent question, "Why NOT you?" Talk about an eye-opener!

Moving across the United States has tested me and my family with some of the most trying times we've yet experienced. My precious family was hard-pressed on every side, and we came to realize the reason God spoke to us about relocating was not for the specific reason we had originally thought. I now see, God wanted to move us for more than a new business opportunity and geographical change. Uprooting and replanting were significant. Sometimes people relocate, but hang on to a Plan B; that's not really uprooting. We uprooted ourselves with no Plan B! I have felt at times like an ungrateful Israelite wanting to run back where security seemed to be. However, I got ahold of that absurd thinking and have continued in faith being obedient through a season of change. I think many people have difficulty going through trials, accepting what God has in store. It's called an exercise in faith.

Jesus suffered more than we ever will. He was born to die for us, and through intense agony He did. His prophetic crucifixion was fulfilled in order for the Holy Spirit, our Helper, to come and do just that—help and comfort us. Christ, after all, did not die so we would be miserable. He died so that we should live, and joyfully do so! When we languish, how much more should we get to the place of receiving joy and the gift of life He has given us? Even though I grieve today, I know that joy comes in the morning—a new day with all the hope I can envision. I think when we feel wretched, it is good to remember what we have been clothed in as

Christians—the Power from on high and it's ours to call on and bring us peace. Without finding peace in suffering, we proceed as irrational and unfounded beings lacking what we need most— simple joy. It is the main possession the Enemy wants to steal from you.

I've discovered my suffering enables me to classify difficult situations. On a scale of one to 10, some are actually a 10, but it helps to not typecast everything like the destruction of a category five hurricane. Not only that, but I suddenly realized that I've been looking at things through a magnifying glass! Some aspects are just not as big as I've made them out to be. Also, it gives me a more sensitive view of others and why I should be able to both laugh and cry with them, starting within my own family. We don't have to like suffering, but it doesn't have to be our enemy either.

> Who *is* going to harm you if you are eager to do good? But even if you should suffer for what is right, *you are blessed. Do not fear their threats; do not be frightened.* But in our hearts revere Christ as Lord. Always be prepared to give an answer to everyone who asks you to give the reason for the hope that you have. But do this with gentleness and respect (1 Peter 3:13-15 NIV).

> But the Comforter (Counselor, Helper, Intercessor, Advocate, Strengthener, Standby), the Holy Spirit, Whom the Father will send in My name [in My place, to represent Me and act on My behalf], He will teach you all things. And He will cause you to recall (will remind you of, bring to your remembrance) everything I have told you (John 14:26 AMPC).

> The young lions lack and suffer hunger; But those who seek the LORD shall not lack any good *thing* (Psalm 34:10).

> Why has the LORD brought us to this land to fall by the sword, that our wives and children should become victims? Would it not be better for us to return to Egypt?" (Numbers 14:3).

Chapter 85

Children Are a Bit Like Time Capsules

If you're unfamiliar with time capsules, they are essentially a container filled with various thoughtfully selected objects often unique in originality, and then it's sealed and buried. Instructions are left by various means for people of the future telling them when to open it. We made them when I was in school, and the art of making them still occurs today. I can only imagine what the people excavating them one day will make of them. It's exhilarating to be involved in such a project, though we can't possibly know how it's going to stir curiosity for the openers of the secretly kept time capsule. The capsule, when found, reveals an assortment of valuables from days past to the awaiting future audience. It's something we can't actually see except in our mind's eye. Sounds kind of like faith. Even so, when we seal that lid, we do so with anticipation of the excitement.

Can you envision what I mean when I say our children are like time capsules? We spend quite a few years putting things into them—in their bodies to satisfy their appetites for a good and healthy life; in their minds to nourish them daily as they develop. As parents, we do our best before setting them free to begin building their own lives. Our son had a mindset for college and decided in high school where he would attend. I remember having a conversation with him before he went away for college. He said, "Mom, I want to see if I can make it on my own." I looked him in the eye and said with mindful and heartfelt confidence, "I have no doubt you will 'make it' better than you ever imagined." I know we've done something right as parents, because he often asks both my husband and me our thoughts and ideas when he needs to make decisions. Many conversations have taken place while he is currently attending college. Indeed, we are preparing our children for their future . . . or are we?

The question is: With what are we nourishing their bodies and minds? As they indubitably reach adulthood, how prepared will they be to greet the inevitable future on their own? I think most parents anticipate excellent qualities such as boldness, intelligence, creativity, and a passion for life, along with other fine character traits to exude out of them. Tomorrow's encounters with our children will be made with amazement at what undaunted qualities they possess. We also hope that others along their path will aspire to be like-minded, learning from them, and by their good example, go on to lead others along an optimistic path.

Amazingly, our mistakes, and we all make them, can be corrected, because God is a restoring God. Thinking of our children like a time capsule is a unique way to consider how we train them. How we love, teach, and inspire them should make our children better than we have been as parents or guardians. Jesus said we will do greater things than He. So if that's the truth, and it is, then we can certainly embrace it and do our part with the greatest of hope.

> Whom heaven must receive until the times of restoration of all things, which God has spoken by the mouth of all His holy prophets since the world began (Acts 3:21).

> For I know the thoughts that I think toward you, says the Lord, thoughts of peace and not of evil, to give you a future and a hope (Jeremiah 29:11).

> And the vision of the evenings and mornings which was told is true; therefore seal up the vision, *for it refers* to many days *in the future* (Daniel 8:26).

Chapter 86

Entitlement Cannot Unify

The family unit being torn apart by a sense of entitlement is something that arises in the best of people. An entitlement attitude is a wedge in any situation no matter where it rises up. It sets apart the doers from the slackers. I've noticed there is no age limit of those who tote around an empty suitcase ready to garner what's outside their sanction. Yes, needs are many but, simply put, an attitude of entitlement lacks focus on righteous behavior. It's cultivated in the work place, school, church, and families. Most of us have walked through a season of extreme difficulty when a "wrench" is thrown in the middle of family or friends. It seems to takes us by surprise. Perhaps if we had been more prepared, we could have placed an open tool box in the middle of the bunch to catch the wrench, putting it in its place before things became unhinged. That's called 20/20 hind sight, because we have realized too late what "should'a, would'a, could'a" have taken place.

Sadly, a death in a family is one of the times disunity rears its ugly head, as if the sadness of losing a loved one isn't devastating enough. Battles arise between family members, especially between siblings, instead of pulling together. Coincidently, a spirit of entitlement rushes in with a self-serving agenda. I've seen precious families torn apart and never restored when something like this happens. Family unity is based on foundational love for one another. Entitlement happens because an attitude laced with greed rises up that says "I deserve something." Executors of wills are hired to disarm discrepancies and put out fires because people have a tendency to revert back to a childlike mentality of "that's mine." It isn't unheard of during family squabbles that the family members do not even know why they want something; they just don't want anyone else to have it, whatever it may be. They simply believe they deserve it. I do understand the pain when something doesn't end up in the hands of the individual who should have received it. More important, I can't think of an instance where a material object is ever as important as a relationship between people. Something honorable is never the result when putting material possessions before love for one another.

A great way to prepare for handling this kind of situation is when our children are youngsters. Some things are just inevitable, we say, but not so if we implement God's plan of relationship. All children of God deserve His good measure, and He has an endless supply. Give your children the opportunity to love one another. Teach the crown jewel of self-less-ness so you won't have to undo selfishness.

> Be kindly affectionate to one another with brotherly love, in honor giving preference to one another (Romans 12:10).

> For from within, out of the heart of men, proceed evil thoughts, adulteries, fornications, murders, thefts, covet-ousness, wickedness, deceit, lewdness, an evil eye, blas-phemy, pride, foolishness. All these evil things come from within and defile a man" (Mark 7:21-23).

> Give, and it will be given to you: good measure, pressed down, shaken together, and running over will be put into your bosom. For with the same measure that you use, it will be measured back to you" (Luke 6:38).

Chapter 87

Expect the Unexpected

When we least expect it, the unexpected comes. It doesn't mean we focus more on ill-fated situations and less on God. We thank God for opportunities that alert us, but because of our "schedules" we would like a little more advanced notice for, you know, the sake of convenience. Oh yes, we're all about convenience these days, but that's just not going to happen. We're talking about the unexpected! For the most part, I believe we practice focusing on optimistic matters and the best God has for us. Even so, at times we find surprises, not only at the door but also pouring in through windows. Look at it this way, even the unexpected is something God allows, because He certainly is not taken by surprise.

When I was pregnant, my doctor wanted me to read the book, *What to Expect When You're Expecting*—an amazing and helpful book. But he made one thing clear: He did not want me to read the chapters in the back where details were written for specific problems experienced in some pregnancies. He wanted me focused more on doing everything I could to make healthy progress. Should I find myself in an unexpected situation, then I would be able to address it with the help in the book. But there was no sense in worrying, which would affect both me and my baby's well-being. That taught me a healthy way to look at being prepared as best as I could for something out of the ordinary.

In personal relationships, these unplanned situations can hurt the deepest. I don't know about you, but my level of trust runs deep, which is why we are not to set anyone above our relationship with Christ, the One who will never fail us. We also should limit those we hold nearest— the ones with whom we allow ourselves to be transparent and vulnerable. When we or those closest to us experience conflict or anguish, walls go up because it's more of a wound than a hurt. A hurt is something that usually only needs a bandage, but a wound is something that can require surgery. Depending on occupation and personality type, we can feel lonely and wonder who our confidants are. It takes wisdom and prayer on a daily basis. We are never alone as God is our ever present "go to." More important, He stirs our mind and heart with such awakening of our situation that extreme and deep healing takes place for both the one inflicting and the afflicted.

God enlarges our territory on a daily basis accompanied by many doors, along with specific keys to lock and unlock them. Relationships are not meant to cause harm to one another, but this greatly depends on what and how they have been established. The Lord tells us not to be afraid; because He calls us by name, and we are His. So when we go through deep rivers of difficulty, we will not drown! When we walk through fires of oppression, we will not be burned to a cinder. People cannot consume us with hurt. He is our Lord, the Holy One of Israel, and He gave His life for our freedom. We are precious to Him. With God as your standard, stay prayed up in preparation for the unexpected.

> When you pass through the waters, I *will be* with you; And through the rivers, they shall not overflow you. When you walk through the fire, you shall not be burned, nor shall the flame scorch you (Isaiah 43:2).

> Therefore I say to you, do not worry about your life, what you will eat or what you will drink; nor about your body, what you will put on. Is not life more than food and the body more than clothing? Look at the birds of the air, for they neither sow nor reap nor gather into barns; yet your heavenly Father feeds them. Are you not of more value than they? Which of you by worrying can add one cubit to his stature? (Matthew 6:25-27).

> Therefore you also be ready, for the Son of Man is coming at an hour you do not expect (Matthew 24:44).

> My soul, wait silently for God alone, for my expectation *is* from Him (Psalm 62:5).

Chapter 88

Ruach: Spirit of God

Today is a beautiful day for prayer, no matter what time it is. Before beginning my daily routine is the time I find to be the most exhilarating. A cup of hot toasted-coconut coffee while sitting outside on our deck taking in the cool fresh morning air is by far another of my favorite ways to start the day. Especially if I have been obedient and left any concerns I may have had where they belong—in the previous day. With the rising of the sun, I am awakened with a clear and rested mind, able to view all things with a new outlook and plan.

The Hebrew word *Ruach* means "the Spirit of God," like breath and wind. What a great way to go about the business of the day, delivering a breath of fresh air and lightening the load of others with a gift of encouragement. Who can't use that? God breathes life into us through Scripture, so that we can breathe life into others.

I find it interesting how often we have to go back to the beginning to find ourselves, casting off the excess accumulation of rubbish swirling around us. Embracing each day is like returning to our first love, our passion, our desire, and our fire for life, deciding that nothing of the past is going to detain our quest. That alone is purpose enough to continue our adventures toward life's discoveries. Resting in that, we can search ourselves and have a fresh encounter with God.

Wake up and welcome the atmosphere of freedom as it sweeps over you. Don't settle on previous encounters with God that you continue to testify about. Make new and fresh encounters as testimony. Like the Scripture says, you are living in the deep, not the shallow. God is the beginning and the end. He surely is present at our beginning and is assuredly there for us at our end. He is the refreshing and the love that enables us to be in the deep waters in safety with Him. When we discipline ourselves honoring the freedom enveloping us, we will find God among us. There are moments we all feel like that formless, empty, and dark earth. That's when God does His most magnificent work of shaping and molding.

My heart longs to refresh the weary, because God never intended His sons and daughters to get lost after He gave them the gift of embracing Christ. It is with boldness that I believe in the wave of His supernatural authority to overtake and overpower any other agenda. We have been given stewardship over our time here on earth. Let's live in a land of rejuvenation!

> In the beginning God created the heavens and the earth. Now the earth was formless and empty, darkness was over the surface of the deep, and the Spirit of God was hovering over the waters (Genesis 1:1-2 NIV).

> Also He said to me, "Prophesy to the breath, prophesy, son of man, and say to the breath, 'Thus says the Lord GOD: "Come from the four winds, O breath, and breathe on these slain, that they may live"'" (Ezekiel 37:9).

> "I am the Alpha and the Omega, the Beginning and the End," says the Lord, "who is and who was and who is to come, the Almighty" (Revelation 1:8).

Chapter 89

The Tidy and Messy of It All

How can two simple words have such a powerful impact? Beautiful and aesthetically eye pleasing does not always reveal an accurate picture. My heart is speaking about the people of the church. One of the meanings of being a visionary is to see beyond the superficial. There's nothing wrong with magnificent surroundings as long as vision and focus are not washed over and vanish as though lost. The beauty of untidiness is when there is no fear of exposing the "mess" that could be underlying. People, who serve and reach out to be the hands of God, lay it all down at the altar expecting results. I see the altar as a fully living, biblical, and functioning mainstay that reflects the heart and vision of the church. One must experience the messy of digging deep to achieve full potential, glorifying God's kingdom.

I think of Jesus and some of the people who walked with Him—some who were scoffers, thieves, tax collectors, and sinners. Whatever He did and wherever He went was consistently about the Father's business. We've all met folks that seem to have it all together. Those having true depth of character will, in time, expose that which is sincere. Relationship and time will always sort out what's "real."

Alma Kelley, a precious mother of our church, who is no longer with us, made a huge impact on my life. Surely you know special people like that and hold sweet affection for them. What treasures they are! She was one of the most beautiful women through and through that I've ever met in my life, and I will always cherish her memory. Even when not feeling well, she presented herself with warmth, radiance, inspiration, and sparkled with loveliness. She became frailer with illness, and my husband and I went for one of our many visits to her home. She didn't have her make-up on or her hairpiece that she was fond of wearing. I was drawn to her, as she was more radiant than ever. I experienced seeing her with a profound vision of who she was. Her welcoming persona was the fact she was comfortable with us and saw no need for any cover-up. Most precious was that I had entered a special "zone" in her life by invitation. Not that I am anything special, she was this way with lots of people, but it was something God did that was special for me. Because of the luminous glory of God in her, she affected everyone around her. Oh how I want to be like that.

I hope today, we will never attempt to be so pleasing to the eye that our heart takes a back seat to our vision. I want to encounter the people like Jesus encountered. In saying that, there will be times I may not look my best, but if someone needs me and I will go "as is." Every time so-called "having it all together" reveals to be tattered and torn, there's a God-given opportunity to walk arm in arm with a precious saint. Someone has an extended hand to you. Will you take hold of it?

> And Moses built an altar and called its name, The-LORD-Is-My-Banner (Exodus 17:15).

> Now when they had come and gathered the church together, they reported all that God had done with them, and that He had opened the door of faith to the Gentiles (Acts 14:27).

> Therefore take heed to yourselves and to all the flock, among which the Holy Spirit has made you overseers, to shepherd the church of God which He purchased with His own blood (Acts 20:28).

> Then the LORD answered me and said: Write the vision and make *it* plain on tablets, that he may run who reads it (Habakkuk 2:2).

Chapter 90

Sadducees and Pharisees

Sadducees and Pharisees weren't big on anyone other than themselves, for the most part, and did not welcome the idea of embracing people of Christ. Measuring all things so that nothing bested them was what they were keen on doing. Religion like theirs presents itself above all others, and they resolved to do their utmost to remove the truth of who Jesus was. They were afraid of losing their bureaucratic standing.

Christ's view, however, was and is the extreme opposite. His Word teaches us each time a bruised and battered person unmasks their unfortunate wrecked life; it's a juncture of blessed hope. Amongst religious people like the Sadducees and Pharisees, those sorts of opportunities were customarily shunned because it crossed the line to possibly being transparent. The act of seeking and following Christ is not intimidated by the unveiling of oneself either in transparency or vulnerability. In our relationships with one another, we are to have the same mindset as Christ.

Achieving Christlikeness is an open book course of action—one that we will continue while here on earth, page after page. At times, we must allow ourselves the liberty to be excavated. Yes, to achieve this liberty is uncomfortable. Discomfort holds a lot of power as it uncovers that which needs to be released; so, we would do well to keep that in mind. We fall again and again, but are never at the same place when we stand up. Advancement is inevitable. As the most broken of broken people are tended to with compassion, they begin to see themselves for the first time as Christ sees them. What beautiful hope this is to see in others.

Religious disconnection in fellowship can be selfish, usually on the lookout for personal gain. In the Book of Luke, Judas went to the chief priests and officers of the temple guard to discuss how they might betray Jesus. His gain was thirty pieces of silver, of which proved to be his end. The Sadducees and Pharisees weren't about to expose their own sins, but they certainly took the opportunity to silence the ministry of Jesus—so they thought. As for Judas, he consented and watched for an opportunity to hand Jesus over to them.

Let's offer water to the dry, deceived, and thirsty of mankind instead of watching them flounder without hope of a future. Let's lift them up so they can see clearly that they can belong to Christ.

> Then Jesus said to them, "Take heed and beware of the leaven of the Pharisees and the Sadducees" (Matthew 16:6).

> So *are* the ways of everyone who is greedy for gain; it takes away the life of its owners (Proverbs 1:19).

> Then the Lord said to him, "Now you Pharisees make the outside of the cup and dish clean, but your inward part is full of greed and wickedness" (Luke 11:39).

> In your relationships with one another, have the same mindset as Christ Jesus (Philippians 2:5 NIV).

Chapter 91

May I Serve You?

"May I serve you?" That is a wonderful question when we mean it with authenticity. Otherwise, it lacks the zeal in which it should be intended and is merely a rhetorical question. If you expect a yes answer, then you're ready for the next question: "**How** may I serve you?" Offering up your sincere intensions packs enormous good measure toward the person being addressed. In many cases, they are allowing you into a region of insecurity.

Trust is an issue when people are in a vulnerable state. Those with challenges are in the process of acclimating themselves to something seasonal or completely rearranging the life they are accustomed to for an indefinite period of time. Reaching out to others, I have seen what miraculous change occurs in the one serving. That's the amazing thing to me. For those uncomfortable on the receiving end of assistance is their awakening to experience what it's like to be known on a deeper level. Those uncomfortable with reaching out are experiencing what it's like to touch another's life in a personal and positive way.

Our family experienced this firsthand. At the end of a lovely summer day, I arrived home with "takeout" dinner for my family. I slipped and fell in our driveway. When my precious son heard my cries for help and found me, he tried to help me stand first on one leg than the other, but I collapsed either way and was in excruciating pain. Several doctors later, the bad news was that I had broken my right leg and also my left foot! This was shocking to my family to say the least. We are a healthy lot and lead full lives. My son had never encountered home care for another person, let alone his mother who was on the go all the time. He was heading off to college in a few months and concerned about who was going to look in on me. My husband, as always, rose to the occasion for all personal needs. I discovered even more what an amazing man I married. My son had a difficult time seeing me in this condition and was angry with me at the same time. After some discussion with him, I discovered this is how he was covering up his broken heart for me. His uncertainties were evident when he said to me with tears welling up in his eyes, "Mom, I don't know how to take care of you." What a precious conversation we had. I said, "Son, there is nothing wrong with not knowing how to do something, but there is plenty wrong with not trying. We have to make the best of this summer before you go away to college, or we will miss one of the greatest opportunities this family will ever experience."

Our family was stretched. My husband and son learned how to serve someone they could not envision being in a helpless capacity. I, on the other hand, had to ask for absolutely **EVERYTHING!** I struggled with that immensely. Our bedroom became the meeting place for friends and conversation, and the front door was always open. My house was a regular "Starbucks." Precious friends came and did everything my family and I needed, from cleaning to laundry and meals. When I advanced to a wheelchair, my church family also built me a wheelchair ramp. As far as my son, I still haven't heard the end of it from him about how I broke both walking appendages at the same time.

Humbly serve others and humbly accept being served. It's God's way.

> Not lagging in diligence, fervent in spirit, serving the Lord (Romans 12:11).

> Then He said to *them* all, "If anyone desires to come after Me, let him deny himself, and take up his cross daily, and follow Me" (Luke 9:23).

> Now that you have purified yourselves by obeying the truth so that you have sincere love for each other, love one another deeply, from the heart (1 Peter 1:22 NIV).

> As each one has received a gift, minister it to one another, as good stewards of the manifold grace of God (1 Peter 4:10).

Chapter 92

Stepping Stones

When I think of stepping stones, I consider the action of balancing in-between one place and another, maneuvering carefully to reach a target. This reminds me of a tightrope walker who carefully steps on what is directly in front of him. Any other step would be disastrous! When our very life is at stake, how careful do we want to be? Don't get me wrong, being adventurous is wonderful in its time and place, and I live there at times right along with others who are free-spirited and like to try new things. My son however, does not agree at all with my philosophy in that area these days. Ironically, the table has now turned on me, and I'm more careful nowadays, mostly.

When we find ourselves in a detrimental situation, every step matters with heightened essence. It's a different story indeed for those who have been there. Trying to skip even one small step on our path puts us at risk of losing our grip on steadiness. This can land us anyplace between DEFCON 1 and DEFCON 5, which is our DEFense readiness CONdition. Stepping stones serve a purpose. They are to step **upon** not over. We have to weigh and decide what's going to be the best approach to travel the many roads before us. Is it best to take the fast and furious freeway, a shortcut, or the sightseers Sunday drive? Nowadays, we depend on our navigational devices to get us from Point A to Point B. They give us choices about which route to choose. There's even an "alternate" in case of a detour. What a helpful convenience, for the most part. Depending on what time it is, road conditions, or what awaits us at the end of the journey, we choose one.

If we take the fast and furious freeway, we might get there faster, but not having enjoyed the journey as much. It's kind of like when the Dad is driving on a family vacation. His agenda is to conquer the destination. There's no taking any off-road experiences except a restroom stop, if you're lucky. You miss a lot on this rapid-paced trip.

Your aim is a task at hand; whether in the workplace, similar to a promotion, choices in your personal life, or perhaps a church or family event. It's a given you will need to glean information along the way prior to your arrival and commencement. The shortcut gets you there quickly, but do you have the necessary information accompanied by wisdom? Skipping over a stepping stone can be the very thing you needed **not** to miss. Here's something to consider: Have you ever been in a situation where you were the one who arrived last, but accomplished the most? Perhaps you were smugly greeted by prior arrivals and maybe even now labeled "outsider." But your obedience paid off, didn't it?

Taking the sightseers Sunday drive is for the explorer in all of us. Enjoy the day and all the splendor of it. You will be surprised at all you see on a relaxed day. You may even garner a potpourri of trivialities that you didn't even conceive was out there for you. I used to love taking drives with my son when he was little. One of things we did was flip a coin when we came to a stop sign to see which way we would turn—heads we turned right; tails we turned left. On our more lengthy road trips and with somewhat of a destination in mind, we discovered some of the most awe-inspiring sights and extraordinary people and animals. One of our favorites was "Reptile Man" www.reptileman.com, which is a little boy's idea of fun to see critters ranging from albino alligators to Amazon size fish and spiders. A Sunday drive or trip was much different when embarking with my husband who preferred an agenda and maps. It still amazes me to this day how he gracefully tolerated my son and me taking a week's road trip every summer with NO agenda!

The point I'm making is that we should all consider where we are going, how we want to get there, and what preparation is required. As we pray for guidance and expect an answer, it's of the utmost importance that we are, at the same time, preparing for our prayers to be answered. If we don't, how will we accommodate what we've asked for when it is given? God owns the cattle on a thousand hills and everything belongs to Him. Here is one analogy I'm fond of using to describe preparation for answers to prayer: If a farmer prays for more cattle, but doesn't build a fenced pasture, where will he put and keep the cattle when they arrive?

Throughout the Bible, Jesus gives us numerous parables with insightful information. I refer to them, read them, and reread them to acquire that hidden wisdom I often need as daily survival tools and techniques. Many Scriptures refer to the use and purpose of stones and how they affect our journey. When we do our best and strive for excellence, our journey will be as it's supposed to be—no regrets.

So the last will be first, and the first last. For many are called, but few chosen (Matthew 20:16).

This stone that I have set up as a pillar will be God's house, and of all that you give me I will give you a tenth (Genesis 28:22 NIV).

Every beast of the forest *is* Mine, a*nd* the cattle on a thousand hills (Psalm 50:10).

Chapter 93

Me and My Shadow

I have never been alone! Christ is as close to me as my shadow. That's a good reminder of how easy it is to call on Him for any reason. I find it difficult to imagine how it was possible for anyone to deny who He was during his first 30 years of ministry. Especially, since many walked right beside Him, spoke with Him, partook of meals together, watched Him heal the sick, embrace the children, and laugh with Him. He enveloped and cherished the lost like no other. Nothing could keep Him away from his purpose and destiny of permanently adopting us.

We often hear the term "finding Jesus." But He's not the one who is lost; it's many of us who are wayward or confused at one time or another. Christ can lose His place with us, but it's not by His choosing. Never will He position himself out of our reach. He does hear our cries for help and knows our surrender when we reach our wits end. Sadly, we don't always hear Him responding and calling us by name. His voice appears muffled to our ears. We fail to identify with Him because of what we are involved in, which perhaps occupies the majority of our time.

How do we identify Christ during those times when He seems hidden from us? It isn't difficult. All we have to do is mention His name, and He shows himself like a protecting search and rescue vessel that's just outside the pale glow of a beaconing lighthouse. There's a dim light in all of us that is but a faint glow unrecognizable by most. Many times we are frail and wearisome children no matter our age, in need of signaling the One who can help us. It's important to remember that we are never too far out of His reach, and His eyes have always been upon us. The Lord is our Shepherd. And, in many instances, we actually do resemble a flock of sheep by our actions. It is of great comfort that He will assuredly go after the one that has lost its way. I must remember it's possible for me to be that one, as none of us are set above another.

In my younger years, I made plenty of mistakes and caused trouble for my family and others who cared about me. I separated myself from where I should have been and what I should have been about. I thought

I had forever to do exactly what I wanted and when. There was, however, a gnawing at me that was uneasy much of the time, but I ignored it. It's unfortunate that I lived with such a selfish spirit a long time ago. On the other hand, the past cannot hold us. I eventually broke free from nonsense that was getting me nowhere. We can and should remember our past and use it to help others avoid pitfalls. Nowadays, I'm more thoughtful, optimistic, encouraging, and in a better position to see myself laced with joy. Times have assuredly changed me for the better. I finally paid attention to the yearning that was drawing me out of where I was and into a life of consideration for others. My life is an unfolding story of me and my shadow.

> The eyes of those who see will not be dim, and the ears of those who hear will listen (Isaiah 32:3).

> Having predestined us to adoption as sons by Jesus Christ to Himself, according to the good pleasure of His will (Ephesians 1:5).

> For the people shall dwell in Zion at Jerusalem; you shall weep no more. He will be very gracious to you at the sound of your cry; when He hears it, He will answer you (Isaiah 30:19).

> The LORD *is* my shepherd; I shall not want. He makes me to lie down in green pastures; He leads me beside the still waters. He restores my soul; He leads me in the paths of righteousness for His name's sake. Yea, though I walk through the valley of the shadow of death, I will fear no evil; for You *are* with me; Your rod and Your staff, they comfort me. You prepare a table before me in the presence of my enemies; You anoint my head with oil; my cup runs over. Surely goodness and mercy shall follow me all the days of my life; and I will dwell in the house of the LORD forever (Psalm 23:1-6).

Chapter 94

What's Your Modus Operandi?

W*hy* we do something is not always *what* we should do. If our "why" is wrong, then so is our "what." It's like this: If we have the wrong reasoning, then our reaction or response will be askew also. We can justify why we feel a certain way then justify what our reaction is. We allow our minds to trick us, and we become caught in a trap of shiftiness. Not all the time of course, but there are certain aspects and situations surrounding us that can unnerve us. It's the abstract part of life, wherein we learn as best we can to live among the human race. We are all flawed, yet continue by choice to live well and contribute to our fellowman.

The best way I know is to look inwardly before I set myself on attack mode. What's the driving force behind that which is getting me so riled up? A friend of mine told me when I notice something irritating me, it's possibly because that very thing I find irritating is in me also! After I got over that news, I understood it could be used as a signal leading me to a specific purpose, which possibly would become one of my strengths. I can explain it this way: I have said in one of my "all about me" days, "I will never be like my mother!" Guess what happened? Finding out in many ways I am a little like my mother was not one of my greatest discoveries. But now I look at it like I am a new and improved model. It's also like the saying, "If the shoe fits, wear it." And I gladly slip the shoe on, because there are plenty of incredible and loving memories I have about my mom. Like her, I'm proud to be a mom of the 50s FOREVER, which is how my son's friends describe me.

Much of what we evaluate is based on something deeper. If you're willing to go there, it's an astonishing journey. It's not an easy one for sure— this taking an inward look. But, the rewards are remarkable because of the depth and difficulty of the trek. To me, it's like being in a labyrinth and trying to find my way out. There's only one way through, and I may take many wrong turns before emerging stronger and wiser. Most people that have shared this soul-searching experience with me find they have an improved sense of clarity in processing thoughts. They don't view things quite as negatively for one thing and they are more patient and willing to bend. The real eye-opener is how we choose to view differently the world we live in. It's not only what we think, but it is also how we think.

> Finally, brethren, whatever things are true, whatever things *are* noble, whatever things *are* just, whatever things *are* pure, whatever things are lovely, whatever things are of good report, if *there is* any virtue and if *there is* anything praiseworthy—meditate on these things (Philippians 4:8).

> Keep me from the snares they have laid for me, and from the traps of the workers of iniquity (Psalm 141:9).

> And have put on the new self who is being renewed to a true knowledge according to the image of the One who created him (Colossians 3:10 NASB).

Chapter 95

There Are No Stupid Questions

What we don't know should never hold us back. It should be the determining factor causing us to press on and absorb as an apprentice would. Some of us are quicker studiers than others. My favorite teachers in school were ones who said: "There is never a question too stupid to ask." There is freedom in being able to inquire. Others belittled students who asked lots of questions. Those teachers made it more difficult to learn for some students, including me. Algebra was so foreign, from beginning to end, and I could NEVER ask enough questions to grasp the concept. The teacher was great, but even so, I managed to pass only basic math class; maybe you remember the class. Sadly, to this day, I'm convinced my checkbook is from an alien world!

Then I had an art teacher that was an incredibly huge man towering six feet, five inches. He sported a mean-looking spiked haircut that was flat on top. Also, he had a sinister laugh. I think he was the giant from the story "Jack and the Beanstalk." One day in class I had a question about one of my projects. He took a look at it and threw it across the room.

Well, I remember that incident like it was just yesterday! You get through stuff like that and those kind of inner scars don't always have to yield a traumatizing affect. In many ways, these circumstances made me stronger. What was my project? It was a leather bookmarker I still have today, and I think it's quite nice.

Oh my goodness, then there was my first job at a soda bottling company during high school. The position was a secretary, which was great, but I was also responsible for some of the accounting—not so great. My mom, oh how can I even say this, I told her I was struggling and might be fired, so she called my boss and asked him to give me another chance!! What a nice man, he did. I was terminated shortly after that. This taught me to understand my son when he said during grammar school: "No, Mom, I don't need you to call the school or go down there." I get that now! Praise God, he is a lot more intelligent than I was and does quite well in college studying sciences of the mind. Our conversations these days incline me to think my son may not agree with my philosophy that there are no stupid questions.

It takes me longer than a lot of people to "get something"—to finally put all the pieces together, to memorize that scripture, or get the facts straight in history. I remind myself there is always going to be someone who is more intelligent than I am. Equally, there will always be others that don't know as much as I do. Everybody has their own "feather in their cap" in regard to their area of expertise.

If I can draw anything from these experiences, it would be to press on no matter what I don't know or who tempts me to think I can't learn. I believe the first item we need to memorize is a fact—to know whom you are in Christ. Be able to always stand up on the inside! Face those who persecute you. Adversaries will always be around to let the air out of your tires. I have learned to embrace the most contrary and problematic people and situations because they taught me the most.

> It is good for me that I have been afflicted, that I may learn Your statutes (Psalm 119:71).

> We toil, working with our own hands; when we are reviled, we bless; when we are persecuted, we endure (1 Corinthians 4:12 NASB).

> My son, give attention to my words; incline your ear to my sayings. Do not let them depart from your eyes; keep them in the midst of your heart (Proverbs 4:20-21).

Chapter 96

Remember

The harder we try to forget something the more we remember it. Do you ever find that true? Think about it next time you try to forget something. I knew of a situation where a lady was angry with her sister because of a hurtful letter she had received from her. For years she could not let it go. Every time she began to have a softened heart, she would get the letter out and read it, which stirred up her anger all over again. What are we thinking when we do that sort of thing?

When these kinds of situations happen to us, it's so much better to walk in forgiveness. Do your best to release the pain someone has caused you. I understand many have experienced horrific suffering at the hand of another. It's difficult to move on, but vital to our existence, enabling us to be free of what seems like shackles around our ankles. The act of forgiving releases us to receive what God has for us.

I am reminded of the pain that Christ must have endured for each and every one of us. God doesn't want us to forget that. This was an act of His Son's saving grace for each of us. When we live selfishly, we are living an increasing distance from God. We may find it difficult to admit that we are trying to forget who He is because of what we are doing or not doing. That's the tug on your heart when you are trying to forget that you actually belong to Christ. It's the nudging of the Holy Spirit directing you to the place of peace and comfort.

Hurtful things are difficult, no matter how much we want to forget them. I believe it's necessary to put them in a place of triumph. When we read how Jesus was scourged, it is the most difficult visual to erase from our minds. The pain must have been excruciating. Jesus' mother, Mary, watched the entire prophecy be fulfilled—the one she knew in her heart was going to take place through the death of her Son. I believe the angels in heaven wanted to flee to His rescue, but it was not the Father's will. Probably, even Satan himself thought for a brief moment he had won. But a victorious finality was the will of the Father for all of us. It was Christ's destiny from the time He was born a babe in a manger. He was stamped with exultation from on high by the hand of His heavenly Father. In all of humanity, the Cross is where our deepest compassion is birthed.

> In the same manner *He* also *took* the cup after supper, saying, "This cup is the new covenant in My blood. This do, as often as you drink *it,* in remembrance of Me" (1 Corinthians 11:25).

> And He took bread, gave thanks and broke *it,* and gave *it* to them, saying, "This is My body which is given for you; do this in remembrance of Me" (Luke 22:19).

> Then Jesus said, "Father, forgive them, for they do not know what they do." And they divided His garments and cast lots (Luke 23:34).

Chapter 97

Denial Is Not a Good Hiding Place

The Enemy wants us to deny Christ at all times. Denying Christ is to reject every single detail encompassed in our personal blueprints! The Enemy of our souls wants all truth to be skewed to the point of being unrecognizable. Sadly, when people know the truth, there are times that admitting it is not what they do. Judas was sitting next to Jesus at the Last Supper along with the disciples. Christ knew full well who would betray Him. Denial here was one step away from betrayal. In response to a direct question, silence can still be a lie. Failing to acknowledge something to be true is, in a sense, making a declaration to something harmful, maybe not outwardly, but inwardly in the recesses of the heart. The Word tells us that out of the heart the mouth speaks, perhaps, even in silence.

The roots of betrayal run deep being birthed in deceit. Residing with a spirit of denial is layer upon layer of denial's hiding place. People are like an onion when attempting to find the truth of where a particular pattern began in their behavior. Each layer has to be removed, unearthing one facet at a time. This one step at a time process ironically uncovers both deception and fact, whichever way you want to look at it. It is good practice to remember that truth gets embedded right along with hurts. Knowingly or unknowingly, it's harmful to God's intended best for us. Instead of hiding we could diligently be in prayer for God's revelation and healing.

I don't know about you, but facing what I know to be harmful to me is painful. The end result, however, is an earth-shattering awakening for my own good. It reminds me of the research I did online prior to my son undergoing hernia surgery. Because of technology, I was able to view the layer upon layer of tissue in the human body, each intricately designed for a specific purpose. Tissue had to be carefully explored before getting to the underlying problem. These tissue layers were extremely vital, some more so than others, and had to be handled with precise caution to prevent further damage.

This is how we are when undergoing spiritual surgery. If we are insensitive and abrupt, the problem is intensified. We just want to cover it back up because it's too painful. Deep healing requires more than a bandage. At the core of my son's hernia, there was hidden physical pain, but it was also a hidden physical truth. Once discovering the tear in the muscle, it could not be denied and could then be corrected. Once a thing is revealed there can be no denying it.

Rejecting Christ seems like betrayal to both our physical and spiritual wellbeing. Our bodies are temples and the Holy Spirit's dwelling place. It is of utmost importance that we take care of our physical bodies. We make choices that can either cause harm or enhance the health we have. Generating good health is advantageous spiritually, as well as serving the kingdom of God right here and right now.

> But there were also false prophets among the people, even as there will be false teachers among you, who will secretly bring in destructive heresies, even denying the Lord who bought them, *and* bring on themselves swift destruction (2 Peter 2:1).

> Behold, I will bring it health and healing; I will heal them and reveal to them the abundance of peace and truth (Jeremiah 33:6).

> For nothing is secret that will not be revealed, nor *anything* hidden that will not be known and come to light (Luke 8:17).

> For physical training is of some value (useful for a little), but godliness (spiritual training) is useful *and* of value in everything *and* in every way, for it holds promise for the present life and also for the life which is to come (1 Timothy 4:8 AMPC).

Chapter 98

Throw Down the Gauntlet

Who said that when we're challenged we're supposed to run? Enemies, like bullies, antagonize and dare us in order to show our weakness or more likely, make us believe we are pitiful and scrawny. So, either we know what it takes to stand, or we better start talking like we do. We're on the spot, so to speak, and hopefully we make a decision to give God our Achilles' heel and receive His muscle. I've been in this place before, and for a few seconds, I will admit I used my best "poker face," hoping I could bluff my way through. I've been in situations where I was taken by surprise and scared to say the least. That being said, I need to relentlessly seek counsel with the One who is superior in strength and status.

When we "throw down the gauntlet" or glove, it means a desire to challenge or confront another. Today, I see it as a metaphor that represents chivalry, honor, and truth. I don't believe those ideals are of the past either. People who are honest and good-willed set the bar high for others who have a desire to follow. We will continue to be challenged by someone else's behavior or ideas; therefore, we need to stand up for what's right. Most of us have God's Word hidden inside us. Those are the times we prayed; Lord, give me what I need when I need it. We open our mouth and out it comes—our defense. Sure, the Bible tells us to turn from the Enemy and go toward God. But, listen; I'm going to have my say backed by some choice scripture before I leave the scene of my adversary. I don't believe I'm an easy target, but I realize full well, a target is what I am because of my love and service for Christ.

When our son was a little guy, we had BIG-theme birthday parties. His parties didn't last just an hour and a half, they lasted ALL day! Sometimes even an overnight campout followed. Other moms and I joined together to prepare food and grog (fruit punch) to serve before cake and ice cream. One year the theme was knights in shining armor. His birthday cake was made by a lady that specialized in the WOW kind of birthday cakes, and she made him an amazing castle cake. There were young "knights" every-where fully clothed in armor and wielding swords (of plastic). My husband created a maze with his tractor on our property for a journey through a forest with epic-era activities along the way. Though I have not lived in the era of Knights of the Round Table, I certainly enjoyed dreaming of these youngsters all growing up to be someone's knight in shining armor.

Like soldiers in pursuit of victory, we can push back opposing forces or trample over them right here and right now while here on earth. God intends our territory to be enlarged and claimed for His purpose. Everything that has not been declared for His divine ideals is up for the taking. We have the faculties to give notice and identify who we are and take an immovable stance. We don't have to shuffle to the right or the left while sizing up opposition. Their agenda is flawed and totally untrustworthy; ours as Christians is not. Giving God prominence, allocates fullness of prosperity for you and yours, generation to generation.

> For You have armed me with strength for the battle; You have subdued under me those who rose up against me (Psalm 18:39).

> Dominion belongs to the Lord and he rules over the nations (Psalm 22:28 NIV).

> And he said to him, Look now, *there is* in this city a man of God, and *he is* an honorable man; all that he says surely comes to pass. So let us go there; perhaps he can show us the way that we should go (1 Samuel 9:6).

> When you go out to battle against your enemies, and see horses and chariots and people more numerous than you, do not be afraid of them; for the LORD your God *is* with you, who brought you up from the land of Egypt. So it shall be, when you are on the verge of battle, that the priest shall approach and speak to the people. And he shall say to them, 'Hear, O Israel: Today you are on the verge of battle with your enemies. Do not let your heart faint, do not be afraid, and do not tremble or be terrified because of them; for the LORD your God *is* He who goes with you, to fight for you against your enemies, to save you' (Deuteronomy 20:1-4).

Chapter 99

Loving God Is a Dynamic Force

The dynamic force of loving God and what He loves is the sustenance and guide that motivates me. So much so I want to embrace others and sweep them up into my arms. I want to turn their heads upward to face the winds of God as they begin to see clearly what was before unattainable summits of accomplishment. Having Him breathe upon them empowers them onward to become the voice that commands authority. What is left in the wake of this authority is the diminishing and destruction of works attributing Him nothing, those things against His goodness, making void His kingdom.

Power like the thundering crash of a colossal tree in the silent forest is what I'm reminded of as I write this. If you've ever heard this sound, you will never forget it. Your chest cavity vibrates while causing you to tremble from your head to your toes. The resounding echo of the impact is everywhere and you're just not sure where it's coming from. Imagine when the Enemy of your soul hears a sound like this and can't discern its whereabouts. This sound resonates with my inclined ear, serving as a reminder of what can happen when God breaks the silence. The voice of authority is a confidence that brings awareness of what's coming. It is also the voice that rescues with an army that takes back what the antagonist has stolen.

Embrace others along every passageway with welcoming grace for wherever they may be and in whatever circumstance. Walk with them in the direction of a life with Christ. This is a planting in the house of the Lord that flourishes along with others in the courts of God. We can never love too much if we love with the purity of God's Word. Love what God loves and hate what God hates. Salvation is the highest level of inoculation to everything rivaling God.

Life is a great deal more gratifying when we make it more about needs of others rather than a sought after self-serving social standing. When we are advocates for others, we in turn discover larger than life potential within ourselves to function in capacities we have never before imagined.

Though I speak with the tongues of men and of angels, but have not love, I have become sounding brass or a clanging cymbal. And though I have *the gift of* prophecy, and understand all mysteries and all knowledge, and though I have all faith, so that I could remove mountains, but have not love, I am nothing. And though I bestow all my goods to feed *the poor*, and though I give my body to be burned, but have not love, it profits me nothing. Love suffers long *and* is kind; love does not envy; love does not parade itself, is not puffed up; does not behave rudely, does not seek its own, is not provoked, thinks no evil; does not rejoice in iniquity, but rejoices in the truth; bears all things, believes all things, hopes all things, endures all things. Love never fails. But whether *there are* prophecies, they will fail; whether *there are* tongues, they will cease; whether *there is* knowledge, it will vanish away (1 Corinthians 13:1-8).

Now to Him who is able to do exceedingly abundantly above all that we ask or think, according to the power that works in us (Ephesians 3:20).

And suddenly there came a sound from heaven, as of a rushing mighty wind, and it filled the whole house where they were sitting (Acts 2:2).

And the God of peace will crush Satan under your feet shortly. The grace of our Lord Jesus Christ *be* with you. Amen (Romans 16:20).

Yet in all these things we are more than conquerors through Him who loved us. For I am persuaded that neither death nor life, nor angels nor principalities nor powers, nor things present nor things to come, nor height nor depth, nor any other created thing, shall be able to separate us from the love of God which is in Christ Jesus our Lord (Romans 8:37-39).

Chapter 100

Imagine Doing What You've Only Imagined

It's a fact; you're not yet where you're going to be. This journey is more than you've envisioned. My sister shared great advice with me while I was pregnant. I asked her what giving birth is like. She said it's going to be more than you ever imagined and less than you have feared. WOW! It was entirely and amazingly like that. She had great wisdom, because she wanted my experience of giving birth to be mine and unlike no one else's. She didn't want me to fear by listening to those who had horror stories and a seemingly great desire to share them with me!

Imagine something that requires yet something more: ACTION. It's the next step if we want to actually see what we've merely imagined come to pass. If we knew all the steps and encounters of our future, God knows we wouldn't do well when coming upon an impasse. I think how we travel the journey matters greatly. We gather tools and supplies, and then put them to use. Some work better than others. We discard, clean, leave behind, and share along the way. We save, invest, help, guide, change, adapt, increase knowledge, ask for wisdom, and plant things for later use. Those who follow our groundbreaking will have a harvest. And guess what? We also will come upon many fields that have been prepared for us to receive a harvest. If you've never thought of how you sow, now is as good a time to start as any.

By all means, YES! Always take the time to look back from where you have come. We need to remember by heart as well as by mind. Look at the fear that is continually left behind, because though it comes, fear does not arrest us. Fear is put in its place.

Embrace those throughout your travels as you rest and ponder. We allow ourselves to cry, laugh, sing, celebrate, praise, dance with exuberant joy, and welcome the people who come to see what and who we are all about. We collect memories along our trek enabling us to paint a picture with stories for our children and grandchildren. We traverse from place to place. Then we pick up our satchels and move on, leaving behind others to their pilgrimage.

I pray and believe your personal adventure to be a strong and impacting one.

> Of the increase of *His* government and peace *there will be* no end, upon the throne of David and over His kingdom, to order it and establish it with judgment and justice from that time forward, even forever. The zeal of the LORD of hosts will perform this (Isaiah 9:7).

> He will appoint captains over his thousands and captains over his fifties, *will set some* to plow his ground and reap his harvest, and *some* to make his weapons of war and equipment for his chariots (1 Samuel 8:12).

> The thief does not come except to steal, and to kill, and to destroy. I have come that they may have life, and that they may have *it* more abundantly (John 10:10).

> Blessed *is* the man whose strength *is* in You, Whose heart *is* set on pilgrimage (Psalm 84:5).

Chapter 101

Needless Extra Baggage

Traveling today by airplane has certainly changed. Most airlines allow you to check only a single piece of luggage, and there's usually a cost for that one. If you do have need for additional luggage, you will sometimes pay a lot more than you anticipated. It has certainly caused me to rethink my packing for a trip!

The truth is I always pack too much. I remember when you could pack up to 75 pounds in one suitcase. I don't think a suitcase that size can even be purchased anymore. If they still have them, at least there are wheels on them nowadays. I've got one of those relics collecting dust in my garage, and it's full of stuff. I probably don't even want or need what's inside the suitcase, for I couldn't say what's in there. I remember on one of our trips to Hawaii, I had my suitcase so full it practically took a forklift to pick it up. And there was no charge for additional weight! The attendants wrapped several large pieces of bright yellow caution tape around it that said "HEAVY." I laugh as I write this, because I can just see the look on the face of those working the desk if I dragged something like that up to the check-in counter today and expected to pay nothing extra.

More than we need, less than we need. What is the correct amount? How do we avoid the clutter? Speaking from a spiritual viewpoint, I say with conviction: "Lord, purify me. Help me to throw off that which hinders me." That's exactly what He does. Let go of things like ugliness of the past, hurts, offenses, and wrongdoings. Vengeance is not yours to repay; God will contend with them. Avoid teaching yourself how to manage your transgressions by remaining attached to them.

Things you've outgrown; leave them behind or pass them on to someone else who can make good use of them. Believers are referred to as sheep throughout Scripture. It is important for us as Christians to tend and care for God's people by providing spiritual food from the young to the fully mature. If you have reached a new level with more responsibilities, then do what God's Word says and equip others with what they need. Trade in your burdens for rest, preparing yourself to better receive new things from God.

Enjoy the new spring in your step inspired by your substantial light-heartedness. Also, people won't be able to say, "Here comes so-and-so with their U-Haul."

> For My yoke *is* easy and My burden is light (Matthew 11:30).

> Beloved, do not avenge yourselves, but *rather* give place to wrath; for it is written, "Vengeance *is Mine, I will repay*," says the Lord (Romans 12:19).

> He will sit as a refiner and a purifier of silver; He will purify the sons of Levi, and purge them as gold and silver, that they may offer to the LORD an offering in righteousness (Malachi 3:3).

Chapter 102

Unlocking Your Kairos Moments

One of the keys to unlock the best a Kairos Moment can be is conversation. What takes place verbally in relationship sets the platform for building and connecting something that cannot and should not be broken. There is absolutely no subject exempt. Conversation is a healthy way to establish an open door policy with others. I believe everyone desires to communicate even though we may do so differently; it's the simplicity of action and words coming together that build a healthy future. One of the best ways to make this point is to share a simple conversation between my son, Anthony, and myself in regard to his endorsement for my first book.

Son: I'm almost done with the endorsement mom. Sorry I've been working a lot and classes just started back and I've been job hunting. I feel really bad I haven't gotten it to you yet. Please tell me it's not too late!

Mom: Not yet, but soon. I'm looking forward to getting an endorsement from my son!

Son: Yeah, absolutely.

Mom: Hello son, I hope you are having a nice day. I wanted to let you know my editor will need your endorsement within two weeks. Your deadline will be February 6th to get it to me.

Son: Awesome! That's great. You excited, mom?

Mom: The fact that you asked me if I am excited is exciting so YES. How about you?

Son: I am so very proud of you mom and I'm so glad you are the woman who raised me. You are very special.

Mom: Thank you more than I can express. That sounds kinda like part of an endorsement to me!

Mom: Son, how are you doing with your endorsement?

Son: It's coming along mom, it really is. I'm trying to make it perfect but writing is not always easy and you know that I care a lot about what you're doing and I want to make it as good as it can be. You're my mom and that means I want to do the best I can for you.

Mom: Sure son but remember I have an editor with tons of experience. As long as you write the basics of what you just said, it will bless the whole adventure I'm on. One of the things I did was write and rewrite until I finally had to say that's enough. I then depended on professionals to correct my mistakes and assist in conveying what was obviously in my heart and mind if need be. If you don't send me something soon, I'm going to give my editor what you just sent in the way of all those great texts!!! Lol

Son: Haha; ok, but I'm going to send you something.

Mom: You better because you know I keep a "mom card" up my sleeve for emergencies and I'll use it!! Xoxo

Son: Of course, of course.

Mom: Hey son. Will I be seeing the endorsement here pretty quick?

Son: Yup, by tonight.

Son: Just sent it. I rewrote it again and again and I finally settled on my final edit. I thought shorter would be better. Mom, you can have the editors embellish it however they need to.

Endorsement By Anthony Sherriff:

Denise Sherriff has been known as a mentor, a teacher, a shoulder to cry on, a best friend, a godly woman, but to me, she has always been first and foremost my mother. Growing up, it was amazing watching her connect and have a natural affinity for people, and I knew as I got older that her talent would allow her to do great things. When I heard she was writing a book, I was ecstatic; because I know without a doubt that if this book reflects only a sliver of who she is, it will connect with and give insight to those reading it. I am immensely proud to call Denise Sherriff my mother, and I hope this book brings joy to all who read it.

Mom (with tears): Son, thank you so much for your encouragement and the fact that you were the one to enquire; "Mom, why haven't you asked me to endorse your book?" To which I replied, "I wanted it to be your choice to do so." What you have said from your heart is perfect to me. I wouldn't change a word of it. I'm sure you remember class pictures in grammar school and how some parents wanted to schedule retakes of their children if they weren't smiling or their clothes didn't match. I never did that, as anyone looking through our family photo albums will notice. Your picture was you at that moment and you could be nothing more real than what the camera captured at that moment; which is just like what you wrote. I love you.

> I praise you because I am fearfully and wonderfully made; your works are wonderful, I know that full well (Psalm 139:14 NIV).

> That their hearts may be encouraged, being knit together in love, and *attaining* to all riches of the full assurance of understanding, to the knowledge of the mystery of God, both of the Father and of Christ (Colossians 2:2).

> *Let* your speech always *be* with grace, seasoned with salt, that you may know how you ought to answer each one (Colossians 4:6).

Chapter 103

Dream Your Dreams

Simplify your thoughts.
The facts say one thing; your heart says another.
The facts say it's impossible;
Your heart says, "Thank you, God, for the dream."

Yes, I believe your favor is resting upon me.
All the facts don't have to line up before your blessings flow.
Cease telling God and others why dreams can't happen.

I've been praying the Prayer of Jabez for more than 20 years.
When we believe and declare victory over our dreams,
Nothing stops God.

The Prayer of Jabez

> And Jabez called on the God of Israel saying, "Oh, that You
> would bless me indeed, and enlarge my territory, that Your
> hand would be with me, and that You would keep *me* from
> evil, that I may not cause pain!" So God granted him what
> he requested (1 Chronicles 4:10).

Author Bio

DENISE SHERRIFF lives in Ooltewah, Tennessee, and is married to Richard Sherriff. She lovingly supports him in all his endeavors. She is also a zealous mother to Anthony, her twenty-three-year-old son, a college student studying psychology and neuroscience.

Those who know Denise say that she has a shepherd's heart and perseveres in finding and serving those who need her. She feels it is her responsibility to share what she has learned. In fact, mentoring is her passion.

Denise says, "Life's experiences have given her the faith of David to slay giants, the strength of Samson to move virtual mountains, and the wisdom of Solomon to make wise choices." Denise and her husband serve as elders at their church, speak messages of encouragement to those incarcerated, participate in City Share outreaches, support awareness of human trafficking, and facilitate a Prayer Force Team.

You may follow Denise and her ministry through any of these resources:

Web Page: kairosmoments2017.com
E-mail: kairosmoments2017@yahoo.com
Facebook.com/kairosmomentsbook